D1515435

Exploring the Environment Through Children's Literature

372.3 BUT
Butzow, Carol M., 1942-
Exploring the environment
through children's

372.3 BUT
Butzow, Carol M., 1942-
Exploring the environment
through children's

DATE	ISSUED TO 120975
8-18-00	Galesburg PL

ILLINOIS PRAIRIE DISTRICT PUBLIC LIBRARY
Hq. Metamora, Illinois

RULES

1. Books may be kept for three weeks.
2. A fine of five cents a day will be charged on each book which is not returned according to the above rule. No book will be issued to any person incurring such a fine until it has been paid.
3. All injuries to books beyond reasonable wear and all losses shall be made good to the satisfaction of the
4. Librarian.
   Each borrower is held responsible for all books drawn on his card and for all fines accruing on the same.

WD

ILLINOIS PRAIRIE DPL

AL5501 120975

Other Books by Carol M. Butzow and John W. Butzow

Science Through Children's Literature: An Integrated Approach

Intermediate Science Through Children's Literature: Over Land and Sea

More Science Through Children's Literature: An Integrated Approach

Exploring the Environment Through Children's Literature

An Integrated Approach

Carol M. Butzow

Educational Consultant

and

John W. Butzow

Dean, College of Education
Indiana University of Pennsylvania

Illustrated by

Rhett E. Kennedy

1999
TEACHER IDEAS PRESS
A Division of
Libraries Unlimited, Inc.
Englewood, Colorado

ILLINOIS PRAIRIE DISTRICT LIBRARY

372.3

To the students of our readers, that the planet will ultimately be in good hands.

———————

Copyright © 1999 Carol M. Butzow and John W. Butzow
All Rights Reserved
Printed in the United States of America

No part of this publication may be reproduced, stored in a retrieval system, or transmitted, in any form or by any means, electronic, mechanical, photocopying, recording, or otherwise, without the prior written permission of the publisher. An exception is made for individual librarians and educators, who may make copies of activity sheets for classroom use in a single school. Other portions of the book (up to 15 pages) may be copied for in-service programs or other educational programs in a single school or library. Standard citation information should appear on each page.

TEACHER IDEAS PRESS
A Division of
Libraries Unlimited, Inc.
P.O. Box 6633
Englewood, CO 80155-6633
1-800-237-6124
www.lu.com/tip

———————

Library of Congress Cataloging-in-Publication Data

Butzow, Carol M., 1942-
   Exploring the environment through children's literature : an integrated approach / Carol M. Butzow and John W. Butzow ; illustrated by Rhett E. Kennedy.
      xii, 163 p. 22x28 cm.
      Includes bibliographical references and index.
      ISBN 1-56308-650-6 (softbound)
      1. Environmental education.   2. Environmental sciences--Study and teaching (Elementary)--Activity programs.   3. Children's literature.
   I. Butzow, John W., 1939-   .   II. Kennedy, Rhett E.   III. Title.
   GE70.B88   1999
   372.3'57044--dc21
                                                                98-43477
                                                                CIP

372.3
BUT

Contents

Part III—Environmental Impact

Preface

It has been said that we do not inherit the world from our parents, we borrow it from our children.[1] To ensure that the world we pass on to our children will be a healthy one, we need to preserve and protect the environment, while also attempting to correct situations such as contaminated water, polluted air, and endangered species.

The environment is all that surrounds and acts upon an organism. Environment, coupled with heredity, constitutes all that we are.[2] The environment plays a key role in the organism's ability to obtain the energy needed for survival. Unfortunately, human beings can affect the environment negatively as well as positively. Solid-waste accumulation, air and water pollution, the destruction of the ozone layer, and the destruction of biological diversity can all endanger the world that we borrow from our children.

The study of the environment—both artificial and natural—has been a long-standing tradition in the United States. As early as the 1870s, school curricula encompassed a study of nature. A compendium of knowledge about the subject of nature study was compiled by Anna Botsford Comstock in 1911. This volume was re-edited in 1986 (with Verne N. Rockcastle) and remains in print to this day.[3]

Environmental education is often taught as part of the science or social studies curriculum. In some areas, it is a separate subject entirely. We take the position that the environment pervades all aspects of our lives and should therefore be taught as an integrated subject. When environmental studies are integrated into the daily curriculum, children can acquire a variety of competencies in traditional curricula such as science, math, history, and geography.

Though environmental studies can be taught through the use of nonfiction trade books, the use of children's literature can help engage students. Literature is an excellent vehicle for teaching all students, especially so for students in grades K–4. Stories present knowledge in a way that children understand and communicate best. Stories are vessels that unite facts and concepts—a kind of glue that holds ideas together for those unable to deal conceptually with the abstract. Therefore, stories make it possible for students to make generalizations about information that might otherwise be too complex for their development.

In researching our other books, *Science Through Children's Literature*, *Intermediate Science Through Children's Literature*, and *More Science Through Children's Literature*, we located many picture books with stories that were admirable in character and also possessed scientific concepts that could be taught to children through the use of integrated activities. We located books that covered the three major classifications of science—life science, physical science, and earth/space science.

After completing these earlier books, there remained stories that could not be easily classified into the major classifications of science. The themes of these remaining stories were not related to subject matter that could be placed into any of the major categories. Instead, these were stories about the environment, stories about mismanagement of resources, stories about persons encroaching upon the environment. They spoke of air and water pollution, of solid-waste problems, and of the imposition of persons upon the land. Other books positively depicted environments containing the natural beauty of the water cycle, the self-sufficiency of the nineteenth-century farm, or a flower-bedecked seaside home.

While the books chosen for inclusion here are science-related, many of them also speak to the social sciences and language arts, as well as to art and music. Computer references can provide students with additional sources of knowledge. Each chapter also contains a language-related puzzle, such as a crossword, a math puzzle, a word scramble, or a word search. In every case, the suggested unit activities help empower children to carry out the tasks of preservation and protection of the environment. Students will thus be led to actions that will enable them to continue the heritage of a borrowed planet to be inherited by the next generation.

Notes

1. George B. Johnson and Gary J. Brusca, *Biology: Visualizing Life* (New York: Holt, Rinehart & Winston, 1994).

2. James H. Otto, Albert Towle, and James V. Bradley, *Modern Biology* (New York: Holt, Rinehart & Winston, 1981).

3. Anna Botsford Comstock, and Verne N. Rockcastle, *Handbook of Nature Study* (Ithaca, NY: Cornell University Press, 1986).

Introduction

In recent years, there has been a trend towards the empowerment of teachers. It can no longer be assumed that teachers will expect to receive a course of study that requires no input on their part. More likely, it will be assumed that the teacher will want to have control over what is taught, as well as how it is to be taught. In becoming more involved with the curriculum of the school, teachers give credence to their own professional judgment about the ways subjects should be taught.

In accord with this trend, this book offers a series of suggested activities that can be conducted in the manner that seems most reasonable for a particular class at a particular time. The teacher must select from a chapter those activities that fit their goals and objectives. The units presented in this book are not intended to be complete lesson plans, nor is this necessarily a sequenced activity guide. Further, we do not suggest that all the activities provided in a particular chapter can be covered in a single unit of instruction.

Exploring the Environment Through Children's Literature is divided into three parts. Part I, "Land," concerns land use and the decision-making process concerning conservation of resources. Topics include urban and rural land use, land ownership, and land development. Topics for Part II, "Water," include the water cycle, the effects of industry on water, the creation of reservoirs, and floods. Topics for Part III, "Environmental Impact," include historical patterns of environmental impact, environmental awareness, forest management, and pollution of resources. All topics are based upon the complex relationships that exist between people and the environment.

Each chapter begins with a summary of a selected work of children's literature. Next is a list of chapter concepts related to the content of the story, followed by a list of unit words found in the text, as well as words related to the text. For example, the word *pollution* is not found in most of the selected books, but examples of air and water pollution are described in *A River Ran Wild, The Wump World, The Little House,* and *Just a Dream.*

Activities designed to assist the students and teacher as they explore aspects of the environment comprise the majority of each unit. Suggested activities represent the fields of science, social studies, language arts, writing, math, art, and music. The activities are often interdisciplinary. For example, activities for the unit on *Brother Eagle, Sister Sky* center upon the relationships between humankind and the environment, a topic integral to both science and social studies. In the unit on *Ox-Cart Man,* studying agricultural land use in eighteenth-century New Hampshire leads to discussions of geography and mathematics.

In each chapter there is an activity that involves use of a computer, such as for locating a valuable Website, as well as an activity that requires students to conduct research in the library media center. Computers and the library media center are extremely valuable resources for today's students. Each chapter concludes with a puzzle and a list of related books and references (other unit books in this resource, other works of children's literature, and teacher resources).

Exploring the Environment Through Children's Literature is designed for students in the early elementary grades, K–4. In teaching early elementary students, we believe that it is necessary to develop a background for students. It is this background, in conjunction with the material and the teacher's method of presentation, that allows a student to construct new knowledge and make generalizations. The interaction of background material and method of presentation facilitates learning and is of utmost importance.

Active involvement, or hands-on learning, is highly recommended for expanding background for students. For example, many activities are outdoor experiences intended to provide firsthand observation of an environmental phenomenon, such as a wooded area (*The Land of Gray Wolf*). In some activities, students work with sets of before-and-after circumstances, such as the development of a parcel of land (*Mousekin's Lost Woodland*) or the effects of pollution on the air and water (*Just a Dream*). In addition, some activities direct students to make maps (*Letting Swift River Go*), collect data (*Water Dance*), or construct graphs (*Water Dance*).

As with most academic learning that is applied to everyday life, the pursuit of knowledge about the environment should not be limited to an emphasis on specific, isolated information. Acquisition of knowledge is greatly increased when a broad range of different areas of learning are integrated. Because the environment includes everything that surrounds and acts upon us, no other topic is more diverse in the integration of academic content. The study of the environment is an excellent way to approach the application of academic disciplines to issues of great importance to people and the world at large. As a field of study, the environment is an ideal way for students and teachers to integrate a variety of topics.

By using good examples of narrative children's literature in the study of the environment, we encourage teachers to envision knowledge as being more than a mere collection of facts. A study of the environment should lead to a realization of skills, such as making observations and drawing conclusions, that bring meaning to the daily lives of students. The use of children's literature, in tandem with activities concerning a broad cross-section of topics, can lead students to a direct and personal understanding of the environment.

Part I

Land

Chapter 1

Land Development

The Land of Gray Wolf

by Thomas Locker
New York: Dial Books, 1991

Summary

Gray Wolf feared that if the white settlers—the Light Eyes—cleared away part of the forest, they would want it all. At first, the Indians tried to drive away the settlers, but they did not succeed. In time, Gray Wolf's prophecy came true: The Indians were forced to settle on a hillside plot of land called the reservation. There they would reside permanently. NOTE: The word *Indian* will be used throughout this unit (rather than the more accepted term *Native American*) because it was commonly used during the period of American history covered in this book.

Science and Content Related Concepts

Forest ecology, economics of ecology, hunter-gatherer vs. agricultural society, adaptation to the environment, controlled burning, clear-cutting, cultures in collision

Content Related Words

Ecosystem, birch bark, Light Eyes, erosion, reservation, producers, consumers, decomposers

Activities

1. If possible, this unit should be taught during the spring or the rainy season of the year, when plants and trees show new growth. A wooded or cultivated area would be an ideal spot for children to look at the new growth of plants and trees. In such a location, mark off an area of about 20 square feet. Have children investigate whether all plants and trees show growth. Which plants remain from last year? Which plants seem to be growing without attachment to any plants from the previous year? Ask children to examine the soil. Are there differences throughout the plot? Is the amount of sunlight the same in all areas? If the class is examining a cultivated area near a building, how does the building location affect the plants? Have children visit the plot after a month or two. How are the plants, the soil, and the light conditions different? Have children write descriptive paragraphs to record the differences they saw.

2. One of the major results of clear-cutting a forest is exposed soil, which can be easily eroded by rain and wind. To simulate this in the classroom, use two pans of soil; one pan should contain soil only, while the other pan should contain soil covered by a piece of sod. Arrange the pans so that when they are watered, the runoff will accumulate in a larger pan or container. Water the pans identically each day and have the children observe the results. In which pan is water absorbed more quickly? Which pan shows a pattern of runoff? How does the appearance of the soil and the sod change after several days of watering? What is the erosion difference between soil that is exposed to the elements and soil that is protected by vegetation? How does this relate to the lands used by the Indians and the white settlers? How can erosion be prevented?

3. The Indians and the white settlers both burned the forest, but in different ways and for different purposes. Divide the class into two groups to analyze how the Indians and the white settlers used the forest and why they burned it. What are the positive effects of burning the forest? What are the negative effects of this practice? What regulations govern outdoor burning in the children's town or city?

4. Forest fires today cause financial loss to homeowners and property holders. How are present-day forest fires different from the fires set by the Indians and the white settlers? Ask a library media specialist to help children find magazine or newspaper articles about forest fires. How are these fires started? What can be done to prevent forest fires? How are forest fires contained and extinguished? How do people calculate their losses from a fire? Invite members of a local fire department to visit the class and discuss this topic, as well as fire prevention in general.

5. Gray Wolf was not happy when the white settlers came to his home. Why did he refuse to give them land in exchange for guns, blankets, pots, and other offerings? Have the class debate this issue, with half the children representing the Indians while the other half represent the white settlers. The focus of the debate should be the sharing of the land between the two cultures. Each side should prepare their arguments about land use before the debate begins. To conclude the activity, ask the children if they think that history would have been different if all the Indians had shared their lands with the settlers.

6. Have the children learn about the trees that are indigenous to their area. Obtain pamphlets or other information from the state forest service to help in the identification of trees using their bark or leaves as a guide. If possible, take the class to a field site to study different species of trees and obtain bark and leaf samples found on the forest floor. If this is not possible, volunteers might bring samples to class. Have the children make bulletin board displays from the samples. Leaf rubbings or collages might be made as well. NOTE: Do not cut bark from living trees.

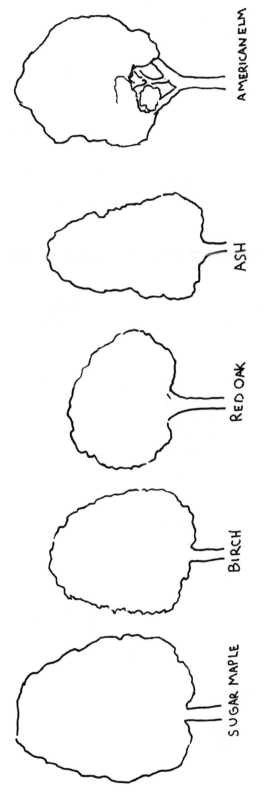

Fig. 1.1. Familiar trees.

From *Exploring the Environment Through Children's Literature*. © 1999 Butzow and Butzow. Teacher Ideas Press. (800) 237-6124.

7. Two cultures come together and clash in *The Land of Gray Wolf*. The Indians are hunter-gatherers; the white settlers represent an agricultural society. In a skit or a debate, have the children present the advantages and disadvantages of both ways of living. Ask the children which culture appears to be more successful in the story. Why is this so? Does history support this interpretation?

8. The Indians knew that burning the underbrush of the forest provided a natural fertilizer for the soil. This helped them grow abundant, healthy crops. The white settlers burned the land once to clear it but did not continue the burnings. Instead, each year's crop depleted minerals from the land without replenishing it. Modern-day farmers replenish minerals using chemical fertilizers. Potassium, nitrogen, and potash are the main ingredients in these fertilizers. Have the children examine the labels of various fertilizer bags to learn about the different proportions of these minerals and how they improve the soil.

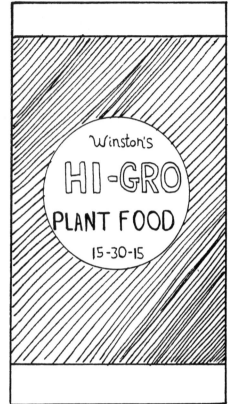

Fig. 1.2. Fertilizer bag label.

9. Use a chemical fertilizer to help the children grow plants in the classroom. Plant fast-germinating seeds, such as beans, in potting soil placed in Styrofoam cups. Divide the plants into two groups. Water one group with plain water, and water the other group with water that contains fertilizer. Have the children check the progress of the plants daily. Is there an eventual difference between the two groups of plants? If other plants are kept in the classroom, fertilize them and watch for any noticeable difference in their growth. Have the children keep a journal or log to indicate the amount of growth that occurs each day.

10. Have the children plan a large garden that has these specifications: The garden is 800 square feet in size. Of that amount, 100 square feet are for potatoes, 200 square feet are for wheat, and 150 square feet are for corn. Carrots and squash use 50 square feet each, cucumbers 30 square feet, beans 50 square feet, and onions 20 square feet. The remaining 150 square feet are for herbs and flowers. Children should make a scale diagram that shows these plants fitting into a rectangle 800 square feet in size. Graph paper will help them fit together the pieces of this puzzle. There are many ways to fit the different crops into the overall diagram. After children have completed this task, have them design their own gardens using the vegetables and amounts of their choice. The garden should be at least 500 square feet in size, and children should label the size of each section.

11. Deer can find food more readily after a forest fire has burned off the underbrush that hinders their foraging. They cannot reach leaves on trees that grow high above their heads. Ask a library media specialist to help children find nonfiction books about the

eating habits of deer. Children may wish to learn more about the eating habits of other animals of the forest, as well.

12. The forest is an ecosystem comprised of three categories of organisms, which help it grow. These are called producers, consumers, and decomposers. Producers are green plants that produce food (e.g., maple trees); consumers are animals that must eat some other living thing to grow (e.g., rabbits); and decomposers are creatures that eat dead matter as part of the decomposition process (e.g., fungi). In a chart (see fig. 1.3), have the children put the following organisms into the proper category:

algae	chipmunks	grubs	snakes
bacteria	foxes	humans	squirrels
birds	frogs	plants	trees
bugs	fungi	rabbits	worms
bushes	grass		

Ask children why it is important that all three of these categories of organisms be present in the forest. How is new soil produced by this cycle of activity? How do these organisms work together to expand the amount of soil in the forest?

13. The presence of a large and healthy resident deer herd can strengthen the economy of a community. Have children list the ways a community can profit when hunters come there to hunt. Invite resource persons to share with the class examples of how hunting can benefit the community (resource persons can include retailers, hotel and motel managers, and restaurant owners).

14. Ask children to pretend that they and their family own a bed-and-breakfast establishment in an area that is known for its good hunting. Have them design a brochure to advertise their lodgings, including information that would help hunters decide whether to stay there. What could be offered as an incentive for hunters to stay there? Children should include in the brochure the name and address of the establishment, directions to get there, lodging prices, and a list of any special services offered (e.g., cable television, complimentary breakfast).

15. Each state has an agency charged with licensing hunters. This agency receives money from the license fees, which in turn is spent to make conditions more favorable for managing the population sizes of hunted animals. Suppose that an agency wants to double the license fee of deer hunters, claiming that this is necessary to better manage the size and the quality of the deer herd. Others claim that the increase is not necessary and that the deer herd needs no further management. Have children discuss this scenario. What would be the advantages of increasing the license fee? What would be the advantages of not increasing the fee?

16. Using what they learned from the book and from other materials that they researched, have children write a journal entry for Running Deer or for one of the young girls of the tribe. They should describe life before the Light Eyes came, or include a description of how life changed after the white settlers moved to the area.

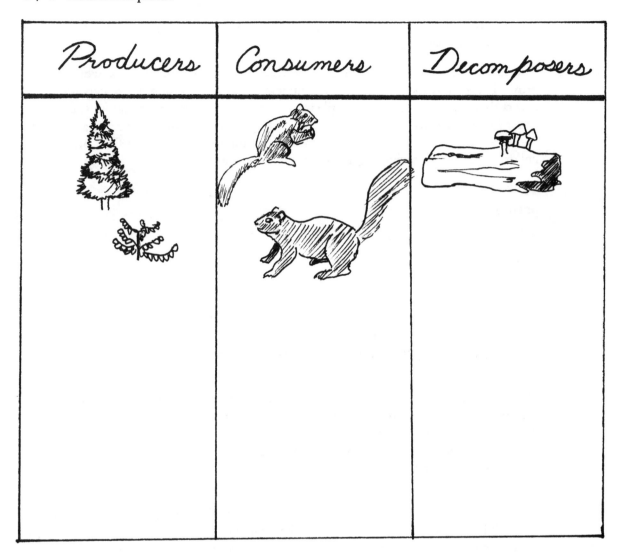

Fig. 1.3. Producers, consumers, and decomposers.

From *Exploring the Environment Through Children's Literature.* © 1999 Butzow and Butzow. Teacher Ideas Press. (800) 237-6124.

17. Have children compare the illustrations in *The Land of Gray Wolf* with illustrations in other books by Thomas Locker, such as *Water Dance* (see Chapter 6) and *Where the River Begins*. What colors does Locker seem to use most frequently? Are the illustrations representational or are they impressionistic? How is light used to achieve different effects? What mood do the illustrations portray? What is the relationship between humanity and nature?

18. Have students learn about Native Americans of today by accessing the U.S. Bureau of Indian Affairs at http://www.doi.gov/bia/aitoday/q_and_a_.html. The article is called "Frequently Asked Questions About Native Americans."

19. In the library media center, have students find information on the Native American tribes that lived in your locale.

20. Word Fill-In—*The Land of Gray Wolf*

    In the sentences below, fill in the blanks with the words that best complete the statements.

    a. To create more foraging space for the deer, Gray Wolf and the men burned the _____ .

    b. When the European settlers came, they offered to _____ with the Indians.

    c. The European settlers really wanted to _____ the Indians from the land.

    d. Soon after the European settlers arrived, they _____ down the forest and converted the land to _____ .

    e. When the Indians hunted, they killed only the number of animals necessary for _____ and _____ .

    f. The European settlers and the Indians were in conflict because the Indians used the land primarily for _____ , while the European settlers used it for _____ .

    g. The two cultures had entirely different ideas about land use. The Indians said that the land was for _____ , while the European settlers said that it could be owned by _____ .

    h. The European settlers marked off plots of land using _____ .

    i. When the land no longer produced good crops, the European settlers _____ and the farmland again became _____ .

WORDS USED

clothing	farmland	individuals	remove
cut	food	land	stone walls
everyone	forest	moved away	trade
farming	hunting		

From *Exploring the Environment Through Children's Literature.* © 1999 Butzow and Butzow. Teacher Ideas Press. (800) 237-6124.

Related Books and References

Bisbee, Gregory. "Building a Native American Drill." *The Science Teacher* 63, no. 2 (February 1996): 40–42.

Locker, Thomas. *Water Dance*. San Diego, CA: Harcourt Brace Jovanovich, 1997.

———. *Where the River Begins*. New York: Dial Books, 1987.

Scorned, James T. "Tracks Revisited." *Science and Children* 30, no. 6 (March 1993): 23–25.

Smith, Patrick. "Heart of the Hudson." *National Geographic* 189, no. 3 (March 1996): 72–95.

Welch, Edward J., Jr. "Animal Behavior: An Interdisciplinary Unit." *Science and Children* 32, no. 3 (November/December 1994): 24–26.

Zucca, Carol, Wayne Harrison, and Barclay Anderson. "Forest Fire Ecology." *The Science Teacher* 62, no. 5 (May 1995): 23–25.

Chapter 2

Land Ownership

Brother Eagle, Sister Sky:
A Message from Chief Seattle

adapted from Chief Seattle and illustrated by Susan Jeffers
New York: Dial Books, 1991

Summary

The words of Chief Seattle plead for a gentle treatment of the environment and remind us that we belong to Earth.

Science and Content Related Concepts

Environment, environmental controls

Content Related Words

Preservation, conservation, deed, rider, compromise

Activities

1. The environment is all the physical world in which we live. Ask children to explain the difference between the natural environment and the human-made environment. Which environment was of concern to Chief Seattle? Why?

2. Have the children make a bulletin board collage of the various environments in which they live. Magazines and calendar art are a good source of illustrations.

3. Have children learn more about Chief Seattle (e.g., where he lived, what tribe he belonged to, what he believed, how he tried to preserve the environment, etc.). For additional information, search the Internet using the keywords *Chief Seattle*, *Chief Seattle arts*, or *Chief Seattle speech*. NOTE: On fig. 2.1, the map of Washington state, locate the city named after Chief Seattle. Bainbridge Island in Puget Sound was Chief Seattle's home, and he is buried there.

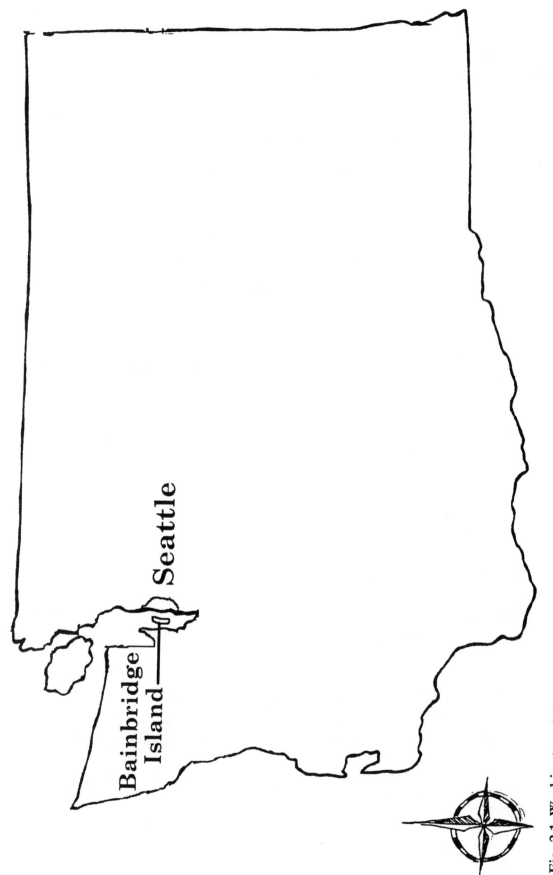

Fig. 2.1. Washington state.

From *Exploring the Environment Through Children's Literature.* © 1999 Butzow and Butzow. Teacher Ideas Press. (800) 237-6124.

4. Have children use the translation of Chief Seattle's speech available on the Internet or the version included in the book, as the basis of a pantomime or dance about nature. Some children might pantomime the themes of the story while others perform the piece as a choral reading. NOTE: Most music stores offer a variety of musical recordings using sounds of nature, as well as Native American music, that might be used as background music for this activity.

5. In the library media center, have children investigate the Native American tribes that lived in their area. Where did they originate? Where did they live? What were their traditions? Did members of these tribes hold beliefs similar to those of Chief Seattle? How did these peoples influence the culture where children live? Are there any remembrances of these peoples today (e.g., place names, museums containing artifacts)?

6. Read through this book with the children and select quotations that might be used as the inspiration for nature posters or drawings. Quotations might include these statements: "The perfumed flowers are our sisters," "Earth does not belong to us," "We belong to the earth," and so on. Children may want to work in groups to illustrate a particular quotation.

7. As the children study the environment around them, they will probably begin to see the relationship between the people and nature. Does it produce positive effects? Negative effects? Have the children produce a list of rules that should be followed to help preserve the environment (e.g., "Do not harm endangered species," "Do not drain wetlands"). Assemble these rules into a leaflet or flyer to share with other classes in the school.

8. The local sights and sounds of nature (e.g., a waterfall, a nest of hawks, some woodlands, an outcropping of rocks) may have special meanings for the children. Ask them how they would feel if these sights and sounds were threatened. What could the children do to prevent their loss? Have them write an essay stating their beliefs. NOTE: If the local environment is urban, children should use the sights and sounds of the city (e.g., historical homes, church bells) as a basis for their writing.

9. Are there particular environmental issues indigenous to the area (e.g., a history of spring floods, the need to irrigate crops)? Are there local groups known for their devotion to these environmental causes? Invite a representative of such a group to speak to the class about these issues. How might these problems be resolved? Will these resolutions positively or negatively affect the environment? NOTE: If this activity generates interest, ask the local parent-teacher organization to help sponsor an evening talk or debate by persons concerned with the particular environmental issues.

10. The character of Marian in *A River Ran Wild* by Lynne Cherry (see Chapter 8) did much work in helping clean up the environment. In *Letting Swift River Go* by Jane Yolen (see Chapter 7), the citizens could not protect the environment from being drastically changed. Have the children compare these two books. How might each book have ended differently? NOTE: These two books are based on actual occurrences in New Hampshire and Massachusetts.

11. The following scenarios have caused much controversy in different parts of the country:

    a. A dam is to be built in such a position as to cause a lake to form. The lake waters will cover ancient stone monuments carved on the hillside.

b. An interstate highway is to be built through prime farming land in a state that has little cultivable soil.

c. A solid-waste disposal facility is to be constructed beside a city park.

d. Wetlands where fish and other aquatic animals breed are to be drained to create more recreational land.

e. A development of expensive homes is to be built in a heavily wooded area comprised of black walnut trees.

Have children explain the positive and negative effects that these changes would cause. Can these construction projects be justified? How important is it to make this kind of progress? How much of the "old way" should be maintained? Is there a way to resolve the controversies? How would Chief Seattle's words relate to these situations?

12. Have children play the roles of persons who would be involved with the scenarios from the previous activity. They should be fair about the issues and present both sides of each issue in a debate. In many cases, it may be necessary to alter the environment, but this must be done judiciously. Also, merely halting a construction project so that no changes result is not always a workable alternative. Have the class vote "for" or "against" each issue after the debate.

13. Many construction projects proposed today involve changing the existing landscape or the pattern of water drainage. Consult a member of the local planning board to determine whether such projects are under proposal. Study the reasons why developers want to implement their changes. Are others opposed to these changes? Have groups of students present both positions to the class and then have the class vote "for" or "against" the projects.

14. Many times there must be a compromise to decide what will happen to an area, such as a historical area of a city, a particular stretch of a waterway, or a well-known landmark. The compromise can have lasting legal implications, such as the assignment of an old fort to the National Registry, the designation of a waterway as a national river, or the designation of a landmark as a national monument. Are there local buildings or natural areas that the children might want to be protected and left intact? It may be possible to obtain a map showing such areas in the local or a nearby community. If possible, visit one of these areas with the class and learn how it is protected and what it offers to visitors. NOTE: Buildings assigned to the National Registry may be restored, but only if the changes to the property are in accordance with established rules.

15. Persons sometimes want to make small changes to their property. In some cases, the owner's deed to the property may prohibit particular changes, stated in clauses known as riders. Prohibited changes might include the construction of outbuildings other than a garage for a single family residence, or the erection of signs advertising the existence of a home business (e.g., tailoring, résumé writing, piano teaching). Two examples of riders from an actual property deed are the following:

> That no building on said lot hereafter erected shall be erected for or used or occupied as a public garage, manufacturing establishment, or be used for any purpose other than that of a private and single family dwelling house with a private garage.

That no livestock, chickens, pigs, or other farm animals shall be maintained on said premises. However, cats or dogs as pets may be kept on the premises, but no outside kennels may be maintained.

Have the children discuss how these changes would affect the environment.

16. Have the children ask parents if they know of other riders stated in their property deeds. Are there any such stipulations in apartment leases? Ask children how people might want to change these riders. How would changes in these stipulations affect the environment?

17. If possible, obtain maps from a local historical society or town office that show how the community appeared many years earlier. Share these maps with children and discuss the environmental changes that have occurred. Are these positive or negative changes to the community and the environment?

18. Chief Seattle calls the bear, the deer, and the eagle his brothers; the flowers are his sisters; and Earth is his mother. This is an example of a literary technique known as personification. Have the children find other examples of personification in stories or poetry, or have them write their own personifications.

19. John Muir, John Wesley Powell, and Henry David Thoreau are among the many authors who have written about the environment. Present to the class (or have a library media specialist or an older child present to the class) short biographies of these writers and discuss why they were known as environmentalists. Are their ideas still applicable today?

20. Many groups today are pledged to protecting the environment, including the Nature Conservancy, the National Audubon Society, the Wilderness Society, the Natural Resources Defense Council, and the Sierra Club. Acquaint children with these groups and their work.

> The Nature Conservancy
> International Headquarters
> 1815 North Lynn Street
> Arlington, VA 22209
>
> The National Audubon Society
> 700 Broadway
> New York, NY 10003
>
> The Wilderness Society
> 900 Seventeenth Street, NW
> Washington, DC 20006-2596
>
> The Natural Resources Defense Council
> 40 West 20th Street
> New York, NY 10011
>
> The Sierra Club
> P.O. Box 52968
> Boulder, CO 80328

21. How do we show kindness to the environment? What is the connection between people and the environment? What is meant by "the end of living" and "the beginning of survival"? As a concluding activity for this unit, have the children write an essay about one of these topics. The completed essays might be displayed in a hallway, and might be matched with the nature posters from activity 6.

22. Math Puzzle—*Brother Eagle, Sister Sky*
    Solve the following arithmetic problems, then match the answers to the alphabet chart to decode the message.

A	B	C	D	E	F	G	H	I	J	K	L	M
1	2	3	4	5	6	7	8	9	10	11	12	13

N	O	P	Q	R	S	T	U	V	W	X	Y	Z
14	15	16	17	18	19	20	21	22	23	24	25	26

___ ___   ___ ___ ___ ___ ___ ___

5+18 2+3   2-0 8-3 4x3 19-4 7+7 4+3

___ ___   ___ ___ ___ ___ ___

5x4 12+3   7-2 1+0 9x2 22-2 7+1

Related Books and References

Cherry, Lynne. *A River Ran Wild.* San Diego, CA: Harcourt Brace Jovanovich, 1992.

Conniff, Richard. "Federal Lands." *National Geographic* 185, no. 2 (February 1994): 2–39.

McLeod, Jane. "From Acadia to Zion." *Science and Children* 28, no. 6 (March 1991): 20–21.

Miller, Peter. "John Wesley Powell." *National Geographic* 185, no. 4 (April 1994): 89–115.

Smith, Shelley, Richard Brook, and Mary Tisdale. "Understanding Ecosystem Management." *Science and Children* 32, no. 3 (November/December 1994): 33–40.

Yolen, Jane. *Letting Swift River Go.* Boston: Little, Brown, 1992.

From *Exploring the Environment Through Children's Literature.* © 1999 Butzow and Butzow. Teacher Ideas Press. (800) 237-6124.

Chapter 3

Agricultural Land Use

Ox-Cart Man

by Donald Hall
New York: Viking Press, 1979

Summary

The seasons of the year set the stage for an awareness of the agrarian economy of the early nineteenth century. It is fall, and the farmer takes his crops to market, where he obtains the goods he cannot produce himself.

Science and Content Related Concepts

Agricultural land use, erosion, organic farming, conservation of land, food production, economy

Content Related Words

Self-sufficient, yoke, embroidery, honeycomb, shear, flax, tap, sap, variance

Activities

1. *Ox-Cart Man* takes place in early nineteenth-century America. Have the children consult an encyclopedia or historical atlas to learn about this period of time in U.S. history.

2. American farmers were able to sell goods to those who lived in cities and did not farm. Sometimes they sold their goods to other countries such as England. Ask children to identify the country to which the Americans sold many of their goods. From which country would they probably buy goods? Help children compare this practice to the modern import-export trade. Do we still trade with England? With which other countries do we trade, for example, for cars?

3. The seasons of the year are depicted in this book according to the jobs done by the farmer and his family during each period of time. Have the children select a season and make drawings to indicate what was accomplished during that season. Or, the children may want to compare the farmer's seasons with the seasons as experienced in their own lives.

4. This story takes place at a time when farmers were nearly self-sufficient. Through discussion and the use of dictionaries, help the children discover what the term *self-sufficient* means. Are there people today who could be considered self-sufficient? Do most Americans fit this description? NOTE: The Amish people, from states such as Pennsylvania and Ohio, preserve the old ways of farming and produce most of the items that they need. They do not have modern conveniences, such as electricity and telephones in their homes.

5. *Island Boy* by Barbara Cooney (see Chapter 10) is another story of a family who are nearly self-sufficient. Share this book with children and have them compare the Tibbetts family to the family in *Ox-Cart Man*.

6. Have children construct a large bulletin board display that depicts a map of the farmer's property. They should indicate the house and outbuildings, landforms, water sources, trees, rock piles, and so on, as well as the areas where the animals were kept and where the various tasks were performed (e.g., gathering feathers, tapping the maple trees).

7. How far did the farmer walk to go to market? Have the children calculate how many days he was away from his home for such a trip, assuming he could walk 10 miles per day. How far was a round trip?

8. On his trip to market, what did the farmer do when he had to stay overnight? What services would he expect to find along the way and at the market? How would this trip compare to a trip to a modern shopping mall? What services are available at a modern mall? Have the children make a chart comparing the trip to market and a trip to a nearby mall or shopping area.

9. The market in the story was located in Portsmouth. This indicates that the setting of the book is probably New Hampshire. Have the children use the resources in the library media center or from the Internet to research some facts about Portsmouth (e.g., Where is it? Why was it settled there? How did its location influence the history of the town? What was its importance in the early nineteenth century? Why it is important today?). Have children answer the same questions about their own community and then compare the rural and urban environments portrayed in *Ox-Cart Man* to their rural and urban environments.

10. The farmer was able to sell all his goods in Portsmouth, including his ox and cart. Ask children why he sold everything he took with him. What items did he buy? Why did he buy so little? On occasion, farmers were able to trade their goods with other farmers or storekeepers to obtain the items they desired. This was known as a barter economy, which is still essential in many parts of the world. Have children discuss the advantages and disadvantages of a barter economy.

11. Was the farmer rich or poor? Have the children work in small groups to discuss this issue. What criteria did they use as a basis for making their decision? How does one decide today whether people are rich or poor? Can the children name some rich people? What would the children need to feel rich? Compare the children's ideas to the farmer and his way of life.

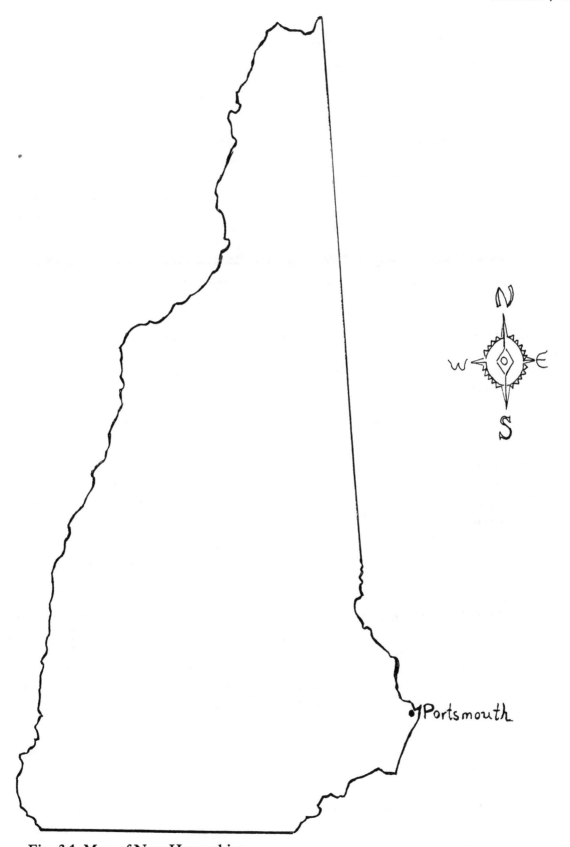

Fig. 3.1. Map of New Hampshire.

From *Exploring the Environment Through Children's Literature.* © 1999 Butzow and Butzow. Teacher Ideas Press. (800) 237-6124.

12. It is necessary to have fertile soil to reap good crops. How was soil fertilized in the early nineteenth century? How is it fertilized today? Invite someone who works with soil or plants to talk to the class about obtaining a high yield from the soil. Have children prepare questions for the speaker concerning such topics as fertilizers, rotation of crops, and organic farming. Why is it that some farmers can produce crops to feed many people, while other farmers can barely support their own families?

13. Have the children learn more about various kinds of farming by having an "Agricultural Fair." Assign each child a particular farming product to research using books, encyclopedias, the Internet, and the library media center. Each child should make a poster presenting information about their topic, including a picture or drawing of the appropriate plant or animal raised. They should also explain how the product is raised, what parts of the plant or animal are useful, and what expenses the farmer will incur in this process (e.g., fertilizer for crops, corn for beef cattle to eat). How long will it take to bring the product to market? What circumstances (e.g., sufficient rainfall) will bring about a favorable profit?

    The following farming products might be researched:

aquaculture	dairy cows	pigs	soybeans
beef cattle	flowers (horticulture)	potatoes	turkeys
chickens/eggs	fruit (citrus)	rice	vegetables
corn	fruit (non-citrus)	sheep	wood
cotton			

    NOTE: Llamas and ostriches, well-established products in some areas of this country, might be optional topics.

14. Most towns are divided into sections, which are labeled according to how the land is used (e.g., manufacturing areas, commercial zones, residential areas, public land, farmland). Have the children study a map of their town that indicates these divisions. In which zone do farms belong? In which areas can animals be raised? Where are factories found? Are there more residential areas or industrial areas? In which zone is the school located?

15. Sometimes people want to suspend or change the zoning laws. Such a change is called a variance and must be approved by city officials, especially if it will affect the environment. Have a town official or member of the planning commission speak to the class about the procedure that must be followed to implement a variance. Once children are familiar with this process, divide the class into three groups. One group will play the role of members of the town's zoning board of appeals. Another group will play the role of the applicants who are seeking a zoning variance. The third group will represent the community members who have statements that support or oppose the proposed change. Have the class role play the following situations in which a variance is requested:

    a. A person who lives in a residential area wants to raise a special breed of dogs. He would have 12 to 15 dogs in their house and yard. The local zoning ordinance restricts animals in his area to not more than 3 family pets per household.

    b. An elderly couple who have a large two-story house want to convert the upper floor of their house to an apartment so they can rent the space to college students and earn money. The local zoning ordinance restricts housing in their zone to single family houses.

c. A farmer who is skilled with machines wishes to sell tractors and farm implements on his farm. The local zoning ordinance restricts land use in his area to farming only, and does not permit commercial or retail sales.

d. A housing developer wants to build new homes in an area where there is a small creek and wetland. The developer wants to fill in the creek and wetland to increase the number of building lots that he can sell. The town planning board has limited development of wetland because of the damage to the natural environment.

e. A home computer enthusiast wants to build a small shop to sell computers in her home. The local zoning ordinance limits her area to residential use only.

f. A new mall/motel/restaurant complex is to be built. The best available land presently is the site of a dairy farm. Mall developers appeal to change the zoning from farming to commercial.

16. Obtain catalogs or sales flyers from a farm-and-garden store. Have children choose several items and do comparison shopping for the best bargain. They might use the farming area they researched in activity 13 to help them decide the kinds of implements they would need. Have children write math problems using numbers and prices quoted in the catalogs and flyers (e.g., Which is the least expensive Rototiller? How much less expensive is it than the other models? What is the cost of a length of fencing? How much would it cost to build a fence around a pen that has a circumference of 600 feet?).

17. Natural and social events affected the lives of the farmer and his family. The weather was one such natural event. Church affairs were social events. Below is a list of newspaper headlines announcing important events that might have happened in early nineteenth-century America. Have each child select a headline and write a news story to explain the event and describe how it would affect the farmer and his family, either negatively or positively.

Flood Drowns Spring Seedlings	Ten Lambs Born at Smith Farm
Drought Destroys Wheat Crop	Barn Raising Scheduled for Next Week
Insects Attack Vegetables	New Preacher to Arrive Next Month
Hail Flattens Corn Crops	Quilting Bee Held for Young Couple
Blight Infests Potatoes	Rain Aids Ripening of Crops
Influenza Attacks Young and Old	Spelling Bee Held Tuesday
Sunny Weather Continues	

NOTE: To substantiate these headlines, children may need to research additional facts.

18. Word Matching—*Ox-Cart Man*

There were many tasks to do on the farm. Match the object to the action done to it. NOTE: Some actions can be matched with different objects, but there is one way to best match all the words as pairs.

ACTIONS	OBJECTS
1. weave	a. linen
2. spin	b. mittens
3. knit	c. feathers
4. harvest	d. brooms
5. gather	e. planks
6. sheer	f. sap
7. pick	g. shingles
8. dip	h. candles
9. split	i. potatoes
10. carve	j. yarn
11. boil	k. sheep
12. dig	l. turnips
13. saw	m. fruit

19. Crossword—*Ox-Cart Man*

CLUES

Across

4. To cut wool from sheep
6. These farmers follow the old ways
7. The market was in this town
9. These handmade items gave off light
11. A wooden vehicle for carrying goods
12. It enabled the ox to pull a cart
14. Liquid tapped from the maple tree
15. A sweet substance produced by bees

Down

1. Used to sweep the floors
2. They were stuffed into pillows and quilts
3. To turn yarn into mittens
5. Roof coverings
7. Pieces of wood used for building homes and barns
8. The source of wool fiber
10. A wheel was used to _____ fiber into yarn
13. The story probably takes place here (abbr.)

From *Exploring the Environment Through Children's Literature.* © 1999 Butzow and Butzow. Teacher Ideas Press. (800) 237-6124.

WORDS USED

Amish	feathers	Portsmouth	sheep
broom	honey	planks	shingles
candles	knit	sap	spin
cart	NH (abbr.)	shear	yoke

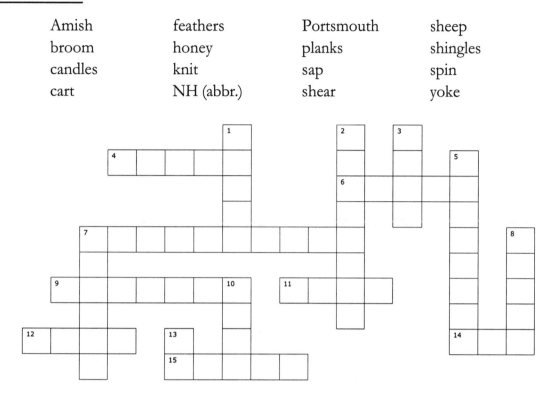

Fig. 3.2. Crossword—*Ox-Cart Man*.

Related Books and References

Clidas, Jeanne. "Personal Plot Journals." *Science and Children* 34, no. 1 (September 1996): 22–25.

Cooney, Barbara. *Island Boy*. New York: Viking Kestrel, 1988.

Hogan, Kathleen. "The Maple Trail." *Science and Children* 27, no. 8 (May 1990): 22–23.

Klinkenborg, Verlyn. "A Farming Revolution." *National Geographic* 188, no. 6 (December 1995): 61–89.

Mairson, Alan. "America's Beekeepers: Hives for Hire." *National Geographic* 183, no. 5 (May 1993): 73–93.

From *Exploring the Environment Through Children's Literature.* © 1999 Butzow and Butzow. Teacher Ideas Press. (800) 237-6124.

Chapter 4

Urban Land Use

The Little House

by Virginia Lee Burton
Boston: Houghton Mifflin, 1942 (reprint 1988)

Summary

The Little House was very happy in the country where she could watch the passing of the days and the changing of the seasons. As time went on, the nearby city expanded to surround the Little House. She was engulfed by skyscrapers and the noise and pollution of the city. One day, the great-great-granddaughter of the man who built the Little House found the house and had her moved to a spot in the country. Once again she could enjoy the passing of the days and the changing of the seasons.

NOTE: The illustrations in The Little House are copyrighted and cannot be used without permission. Instead we have given you a different house that we hope you will like. *The Authors.*

Science and Content Related Concepts

Change, passage of time, seasons of the year, vegetation, land use, property ownership, transportation, distance, urban migration, building use, building sites, population density, pollution, architectural styles, preservation, house relocation

Content Related Words

Urban, rural, migration, population density, architecture, ownership, deed, abstract, pollution, smog, waning moon, waxing moon, new moon, full moon

Activities

1. What does it mean to be a great-great-granddaughter like the girl in the story? Have each child make a family tree using figure 4.1. All children will not be able to complete a family tree back several generations, but the process is the most important aspect of this activity. What relatives comprise the lineage back to great-great-grandparents? NOTE: Sensitivity to each child's family situation must be observed with this project, and no child should be put into a position of embarrassment.

25

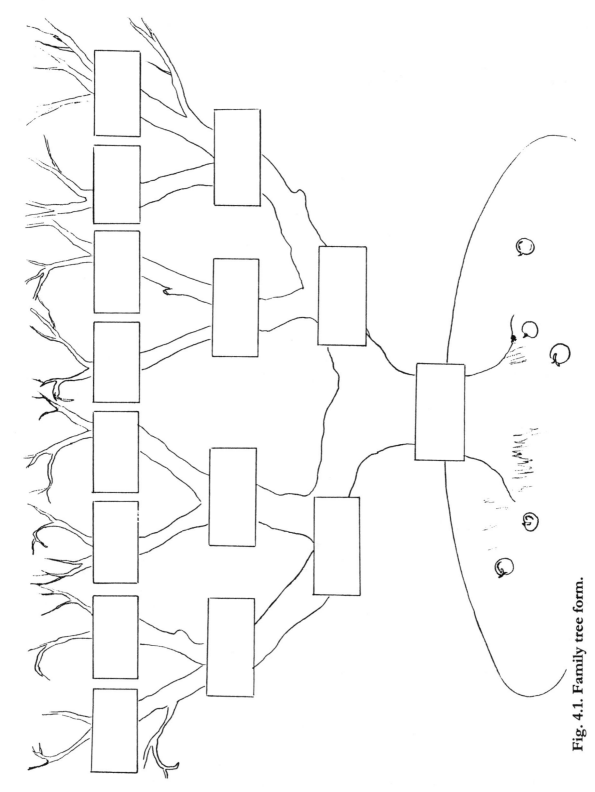

Fig. 4.1. Family tree form.

From *Exploring the Environment Through Children's Literature.* © 1999 Butzow and Butzow. Teacher Ideas Press. (800) 237-6124.

2. Have children collect old photos from their families to show how various aspects of life (e.g., fashions, hair styles, transportation) change over time, going back as many years as possible. Children should date the photos and sequence them in a chronological bulletin board display.

3. To show the passing of a day, locate a window in the school that allows observation of the sun's position from early morning to late afternoon. Without looking directly at the sun, use a water-soluble pen to mark the position of the sun on the window and to record the time of that marking. Continue marking the position of the sun throughout the day at intervals of one hour. Discuss with children the relationship between the brightness of the sun and the position of the sun overhead. What path does the sun follow? What other inferences or predictions can children make after charting the path of the sun? NOTE: Another book that nicely portrays the passing of a day is *The Grouchy Lady-bug* by Eric Carle.

Fig. 4.2. Charting the sun.

4. Choose a specific hour of the evening when the moon will be visible. Have children observe the moon and draw a picture of what they see at this time each evening for about a month. They should keep these drawings in chronological order to show the waning and waxing of the moon. Check a calendar or the current issue of *Science and Children* for the dates of the new moon and the full moon. NOTE: This activity is best done during the late autumn and early winter, when days are shorter and the moon is more easily seen.

5. Have children use maps of their town or city to trace its development over a period of many years. Children should note the years represented by the maps and then collect evidence to help answer these questions: Are there changes in land use? How do the street patterns change? How far is the center of the city from rural areas? Have open areas such as parks changed? Is there a change in water flow of rivers and streams (dams, canals, etc.)? What public buildings are indicated? Is there a change in the use of commercial buildings? Are any structures or transportation systems (e.g., railroad) being built during this time period? Is there evidence that other buildings have been demolished? NOTE: Rural areas are defined as places that are predominantly agricultural in nature.

ILLINOIS PRAIRIE DISTRICT LIBRARY

6. Collect historical postcards showing the downtown area of the community. Have children compare them to pictures of the same buildings taken in different years. Have the buildings changed? What new structures have been built? What buildings have been demolished? What other things in the photos (e.g., automobiles, clothing, vegetation) have changed?

7. Have children make drawings that compare their neighborhood with one where they previously lived. If some children have not moved, suggest that they draw their observations of an area they often visit (e.g., Grandma's house, Uncle Bill's farm). Have the children write brief descriptions of their drawings. Do they show changes in land use, population density, transportation, vegetation, pollution, and so on?

8. Seasonal changes can be observed in many works of children's literature. Two such books include *In Coal Country* by Judith Hendershot and *Red Leaf, Yellow Leaf* by Lois Ehlert. Ask a library media specialist to help children collect these and other books showing seasonal changes. Have children compare the changes discussed in these books with the changes or lack of changes in the children's lives.

9. Have children show the changing of the seasons through one or more of these projects: Make drawings of the seasons or compare two seasons. Assemble a collection of items indicative of a particular season (e.g., autumn leaves). Make a poster showing pictures of various kinds of clothing worn during the seasons. Using figures 4.3a–d, create paper dolls with clothing indicative of particular seasons (e.g., winter parkas, raincoats, bathing suits).

10. What changes in transportation did the Little House observe over the years? In the library media center, have children research various forms of transportation indicative of various periods. How are today's vehicles different from vehicles of the past? How do contemporary vehicles differ from one another? With cars, for example, children should evaluate such criteria as size, amount of metal trim, axle height, size of windshield, number and position of doors, and shape of fenders. Have children choose appropriate criteria for comparing other types of vehicles, such as trains, planes, trucks, and buses.

11. Take children to visit some historical buildings or areas of their town. How old are the buildings in this area? For what purposes were the buildings erected? Have the purposes for the buildings changed over the years? Have the buildings been restored or converted? For example, an old courthouse may have become a bank; a train station may have become a restaurant. How were such restorations and conversions accomplished?

12. Why was the Little House abandoned? Have the children write stories to explain their thoughts, or have groups of children discuss the topic and collaborate to provide an answer.

13. Can pollution be seen? Make dirt collectors to catch particles suspended in the air: Staple 5-by-5-inch squares of clear contact paper to pieces of cardboard or wood (the sticky side of the paper must be exposed to the air). Have the children set the squares in outdoor places where they think pollution might exist. Leave the squares exposed to the air for a predetermined number of days—usually about 5 days. Collect the squares and examine the "pollution" that has been collected. Is the pollution heaviest where predicted? What areas have little or no pollution? What is the source of the pollution? What other inferences and predictions can children make after studying the squares?

Text continues on page 33.

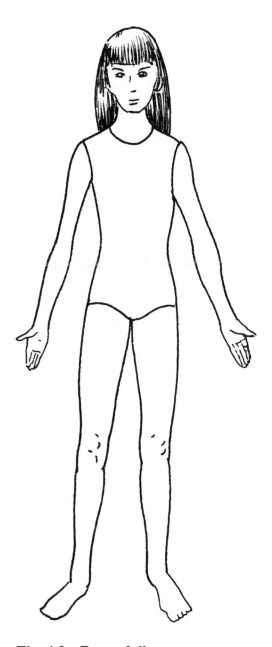 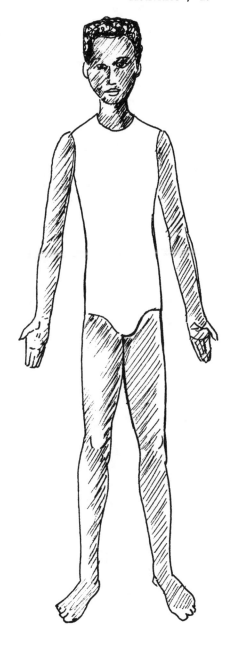

 Fig. 4.3a. Paper dolls.

From *Exploring the Environment Through Children's Literature*. © 1999 Butzow and Butzow. Teacher Ideas Press. (800) 237-6124.

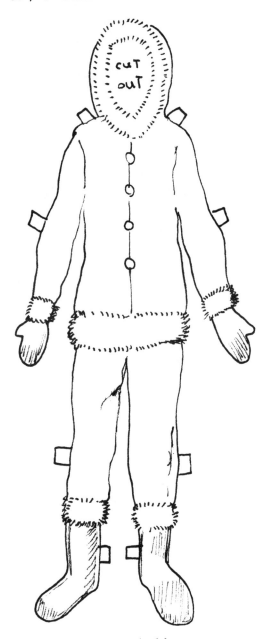

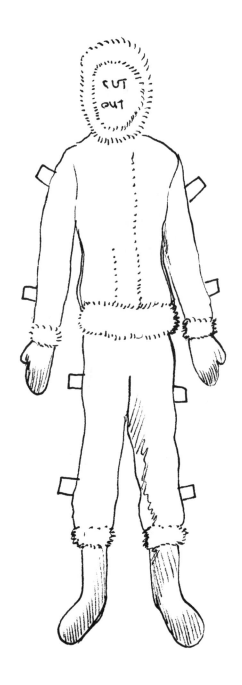

Fig. 4.3b. Winter clothing.

From *Exploring the Environment Through Children's Literature.* © 1999 Butzow and Butzow. Teacher Ideas Press. (800) 237-6124.

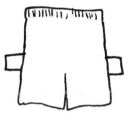

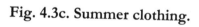

Fig. 4.3c. Summer clothing.

From *Exploring the Environment Through Children's Literature.* © 1999 Butzow and Butzow. Teacher Ideas Press. (800) 237-6124.

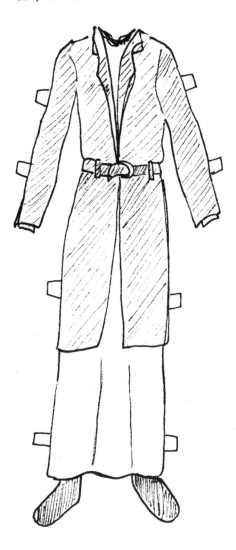

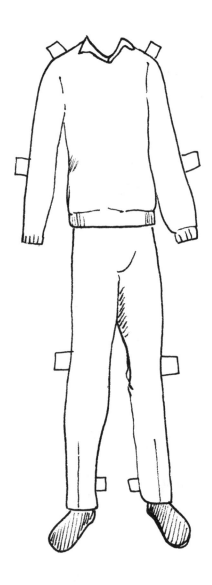

Fig. 4.3d. Night clothing.

From *Exploring the Environment Through Children's Literature.* © 1999 Butzow and Butzow. Teacher Ideas Press. (800) 237-6124.

14. As the human population density increased, the Little House became more and more unhappy. She preferred plants and animals to crowds of people. Have the children pretend to be a skyscraper that has the opposite problem—sadness when surrounded by plants and animals; a preference for crowds and bustle of the city. Have children explore this scenario by writing stories about the skyscraper.

Fig. 4.4. Skyscrapers.

15. Sequencing is an important skill. Have children practice their sequencing abilities by correctly ordering the events in life of the Little House. Write the events listed below on separate cutout copies of the Little House (see fig. 4.5). Have children arrange the cutouts to form the proper sequence.

a. A horse and buggy drive by.

b. The Little House is moved to the country.

c. Gas stations and small houses are built.

d. The Little House lives in the country.

e. Elevated trains travel back and forth.

f. City lights shine in the distance.

g. Trolley cars pass in front of the Little House.

h. Skyscrapers surround the Little House.

i. Apartment houses and street lamps appear.

j. A paved road is built.

16. Have children work in cooperative groups to create a large mural, model, or aerial view of a city. Each group's major task is to decide what to include in the city and where to locate it in respect to other buildings (e.g., Should the bank be located near stores or near the elementary school? Should large parking lots be in the historical district or near the baseball stadium?).

17. Houses can sometimes be moved from one place to another. Invite a guest speaker who runs a business of this type to speak to the class about how this is done. Before the visit, have teams of children simulate the ways in which houses could be moved, using familiar objects such as pencils and rulers to move shoe boxes filled with rocks. Have children research the names and purpose of the six simple machines (wheel and axle, lever, wedge, pulley, screw, and inclined plane) and describe how they would assist the house mover in their task. Another story containing information about simple machines is *The Ice Horse* by Candace Christiansen.

18. Upon buying something at a store, the purchaser receives a sales slip. Upon buying a house, a lot of land, or a building, the purchaser receives a deed of ownership. The history of this property is included in a section of the deed called an abstract. Present the abstract on page 35 to the children and ask them what they can determine about the property described.

19. Based on the example in the previous activity, have children create an abstract for the Little House and her new owner.

20. Have children write a thank-you letter from the Little House to the great-great-granddaughter who had the house moved out into the country.

21. Have children help the Little House find her way home from the city in the maze (fig. 4.6 on page 36).

Text continues on page 37.

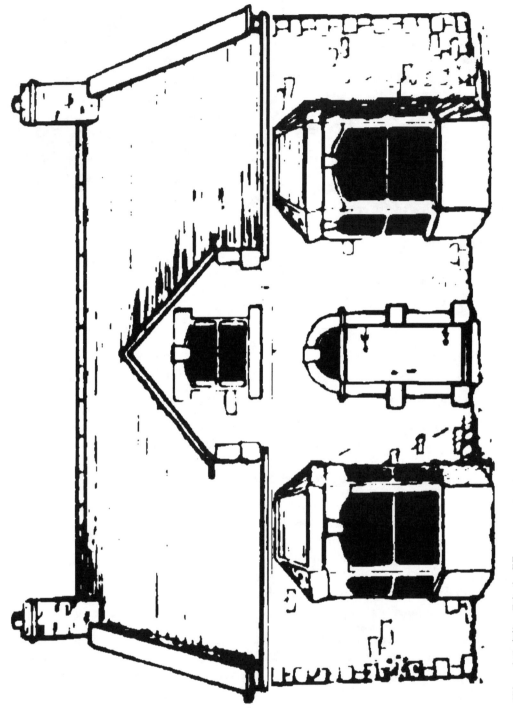

Fig. 4.5. The Little House cutout.

From *Exploring the Environment Through Children's Literature.* © 1999 Butzow and Butzow. Teacher Ideas Press. (800) 237-6124.

A

<u>Abstract of the Title</u>

<u>of</u>

<u>Evi Fuller</u>

All that tract or parcel of land situated in the town of
Olean, county of Cattaraugus and the state of New York
distinguished by part of Lot #5, section #4, town #1,
range #4 of the Holland Land Company's survey bounded and
described as follows: Commencing at a point in the center
line of King Street, 9 chains and 74 links, northerly
from the point where the said center line is intersected
by the center line of Railroad Avenue: thence northerly
on the center line of said King Street 2 chains, 92½
links; thence easterly at right angles with the center of
the street 4 chains; thence southerly with a line paral-
lel with the center line of King Street 2 chains, 57½
links to the north line of Brook Street; thence westerly
along the north line of Brook Street to the place of beginning. Exempting 24 feet 9 inches from the west side
for a street.

> Cuba National Bank conveys these premises to Albert S.
>   Sloan June 17, 1880
> Albert S. Sloan to Mary A. Miller October 26, 1881
> Mary A. Miller to Lucy J. Sloan November 3, 1881
> Lucy J. Sloan to Sara Bentley January 8, 1883
> Sara Bentley to Andrew J. Walsh April 29, 1887
> Andrew J. Walsh to George Stater January 22, 1890
> George Stater to Evi Fuller March 20, 1902
> Evi Fuller to Hannah Yard September 19, 1913
> Hannah Yard to Frederick Olds August 1, 1916
> Frederick Olds (died) to Miranda Olds October 26, 1921
> Miranda Olds to Robert Weatherall, Sr. August 14, 1923
> Robert Weatherall, Sr. (died) to Robert Weatherall, Jr.
>   January 30, 1946
> Robert Weatherall, Jr. to Joseph Hollander September
>   24, 1948

NOTE: The Hollander family is still in possession of said property.

The Little House Maze

Start

Fig. 4.6. *The Little House* **maze.**

From *Exploring the Environment Through Children's Literature.* © 1999 Butzow and Butzow. Teacher Ideas Press. (800) 237-6124.

22. Using a paintbrush program on the computer, design a "Little House" of your own. Print a copy for a bulletin board display.

23. Read ads in the newspaper about houses for sale. What information can you find—number of bedrooms, location, lot size, cost, etc.? Make up your own description advertising a house for sale—perhaps the one you designed.

Related Books and References

Carle, Eric. *The Grouchy Ladybug*. New York: Thomas Y. Crowell, 1977.

Christiansen, Candace. *The Ice Horse*. Illustrated by Thomas Locker. New York: Dial Books, 1993.

Ehlert, Lois. *Red Leaf, Yellow Leaf*. San Diego, CA: Harcourt Brace Jovanovich, 1991.

Hendershot, Judith. *In Coal Country*. New York: Alfred A. Knopf, 1987.

Chapter 5

Patterns of Movement

Earthdance

by Joanne Ryder
New York: Henry Holt, 1996

Summary

Like the seasons that reappear every year, our lives follow patterns of movement.

Science and Content Related Concepts

Earthdance, movement of Earth, population density, humanity

Content Related Words

Motion, growth, imagination, pantomime, transportation

Activities

1. Have the children choreograph their own concept of the Earthdance. Some of the action words that appear in the story will be helpful in creating this dance: *running, hopping, dancing, leaping, stretching, spinning, growing, twirling, tumbling, murmuring, shaking, wiggling, talking, laughing, singing, humming,* and *resting.*

    A story will need to be written as the first step in choreographing the Earthdance. Then it would be helpful to engage the talents of a gym teacher or someone who knows about modern dance to help design the Earthdance motions. Finally, a music teacher might assist in adapting some music for this event.

2. A dance is rhythmic movement. The actions of this rhythmic movement are repeated at particular intervals and in particular patterns. Have an older child or an adult experienced in dance teach the class some dance patterns. Ask this individual how the various motions are combined to form a dance (e.g., the waltz, the two step, the line dance). Are there modern dances that do not repeat the motions of the rhythmic movement at particular intervals or in particular patterns? Have the class try performing some modern dancing to determine if this is true. Can they invent a patterned, predictable dance? Can they invent an unpatterned, unpredictable dance?

3. To help children learn more about rhythms and patterns, invite to class someone with a keyboard synthesizer. What various rhythms can the synthesizer produce? Are they fast or slow? Do they represent the music of different countries? Have the class clap the

rhythms as they listen. Ask children which rhythms they feel best convey places on Earth (e.g., mountains, lakes, plains). Have the children clap rhythms of their own to represent events in their lives.

4. When things move in nature, visible change often occurs (e.g., when clouds move, the weather changes; when Earth rotates, day and night occur). Are there other examples of this cause-and-effect relationship in nature? To introduce children to a discussion of this topic, have them discuss cause and effect in their lives (e.g., What happens if they forget their lunch money? What happens if they get an A on their math test?).

5. Changes in the weather can also be cyclic, taking various forms (e.g., flooding of the Nile River in Egypt, snow in the Swiss Alps, monsoons in India, El Niño storms in California). Ask children how these weather forms affect the climate and culture of the places where they occur. How would the places be different if these weather patterns did not occur?

6. People are always in motion. Even sitting very still, the body continues the movements necessary for breathing and to stay alive. People pattern their movements by the time of day, the day of the week, and the seasons of the year. Have children discuss this. For example, if it were 8 A.M., they would probably be going to school; if it were a Saturday during the summer, they might be hiking in the woods or playing with friends. Ask children how else time, date, and seasons influence their movements? How do time, date, and seasons affect the Earthdance that is always in motion?

7. People are creatures of voluntary patterns of motion. Ask children to identify various types of voluntary movement that people exhibit (e.g., running down a soccer field, delivering newspapers from a bike, taking a walk, practicing the clarinet, going to church). Have children draw pictures of themselves performing an action or pattern and describe what they are doing in the pictures.

8. Some occupations involve a natural rhythm based on time (e.g., fishermen, business commuters, truck drivers, school teachers). Their actions are controlled by daily patterns. Have children think of other occupations with patterns that depend upon the clock.

9. Earth is our home, and all people are part of its dance. Each person, though, has a special "home" on this Earth. Have children draw pictures portraying what "home" is for them (e.g., a place where they can slide down hills in the winter, a place where they have a special tree house, a shortcut route to a friend's house).

10. The people portrayed on the front cover of *Earthdance* are all in their cars going somewhere. Ask children how they determine the best way to go when planning a trip. How do they find the section of town they want to visit, or the street that is their destination? Have children access Map Quest on the Internet at www.mapquest.com. If they provide their present location and desired destination, Map Quest will supply detailed directions and maps for the trip.

11. Have children make an Earthdance quilt by combining pictures, geometric designs, or cloth quilt squares. It is also possible to make a small quilt using photographs or silhouettes of all the children in the class. Using cloth quilt squares will require the most time but will result in the nicest product, which can be displayed in the school, given to a special person, and so on.

12. Have children create their own animated motion. Using a small notebook with many pages that can be flipped through with the fingers, draw a series of pictures—one in the corner of each sheet. Change each picture slightly so that when the pages are flipped through, the drawing appears to move. Have children compare this animation to cartoon animation in movies.

Fig. 5.1. Flip-book figures.

From *Exploring the Environment Through Children's Literature.* © 1999 Butzow and Butzow. Teacher Ideas Press. (800) 237-6124.

13. The actions or movements of people greatly affect the environment. Below is a list of several actions that affect the environment, either for better or worse. Have each child select one of the actions and write a story about the changes that will occur (e.g., building a road might disrupt the natural environment, yet it might make it easier for children to visit their grandparents).

Damming a river for flood control	Clear-cutting 80 acres of forest for house lots
Cutting down Christmas trees	Constructing a long fishing pier over a saltwater bay
Creating a sanitary landfill	Seeding a new lawn
Pruning a group of overgrown lilac bushes	Creating a footpath or boardwalk in the Everglades
Dredging out a beach site in a lake	Offering tax incentives for restoring historic houses
Establishing a wildlife refuge	Installing new systems for reducing pollution waste from factories
Erecting a four-lane bridge	Joining a club whose members pick up road litter
Building a fast-food restaurant in a seaside village	Bulldozing several vacant acres of land to build a mini-mall

14. The word *Earthdance* implies that the population is always in motion, or always growing. Ask a library media specialist to help children determine the most populated cities and countries on Earth. What are the fastest-growing cities and countries? Do the two lists overlap? What are the problems inherent to these increases in population?

15. Joanne Ryder is the author of this book and several others in which children are asked to imagine that they are an animal (e.g., a chipmunk, a snail, a humpbacked whale). Share some of Ryder's other books with the children. Ask them what kind of animal they would like to be, why, and what they think it would be like to be this animal. Have children write a story about the animal using a style similar to Ryder's.

16. Have the children invent a new animal and the environment in which it lives. Have them draw a picture of the imaginary animal and write a brief description of it and its environment, then pretend to be this animal and write a story using a style similar to Joanne Ryder's.

17. Joanne Ryder, who wrote *Earthdance*, lives in Pacific Grove, California, very close to the Pacific Ocean; she is married to Lawrence Yep, another children's author). Have children find more information about Joanne Ryder in the library media center. NOTE: Up-to-date biographic encyclopedias should give children adequate information when researching children's authors.

18. *People* by Peter Spier is an interesting book to compare to *Earthdance*. Share this book with the children and discuss Spier's convictions about people. What problems might occur as the population continues to expand? Does he consider people to be in motion, too? What kinds of environments does he portray?

19. Math Puzzle—*Earthdance*
    Solve the following arithmetic problems, then match the answers to the alphabet chart to decode the message.

A	B	C	D	E	F	G	H	I	J	K	L	M
1	2	3	4	5	6	7	8	9	10	11	12	13

N	O	P	Q	R	S	T	U	V	W	X	Y	Z
14	15	16	17	18	19	20	21	22	23	24	25	26

_____   _____   _____   _____   _____   _____

3x2   5x3   6x3   25+0   10+5   7x3

_____   _____   _____   _____   _____   _____   _____;

1+0   9x2   3+2   4x2   7+8   11+2   4+1

_____   _____   _____   _____   _____   _____

12+13   12+3   15+6   5-4   12+6   2+3

_____   _____   _____   _____   _____   _____   _____   _____

4x4   10+8   10-5   6-3   3x3   3x5   11+10   15+4

_____   _____   _____   _____   _____.

4+1   1x1   9+9   25-5   6+2

From *Exploring the Environment Through Children's Literature*. © 1999 Butzow and Butzow. Teacher Ideas Press. (800) 237-6124.

Related Books and References

Brouse, Deborah. "Population Growth: Stretching the Limits." *Science and Children* 27, no. 5 (February 1990): 23–25.

Ryder, Joanne. *Chipmunk Song.* New York: Lodestar Books, 1992.

———. *The Snail's Spell.* New York: Viking, 1988.

———.*Winter Whale.* New York: William Morrow, 1991.

Spier, Peter. *People.* New York: Bantam Doubleday Dell, 1980.

Part II

Water

Chapter 6

The Water Cycle

Water Dance

by Thomas Locker
San Diego, CA: Harcourt Brace Jovanovich, 1997

Summary

The water cycle is a part of everyday existence and makes life possible. As water goes through its cycle it appears as clouds, waterfalls, lakes, rivers, oceans, and then clouds again in a continuous process of providing water to the Earth.

Science and Content Related Concepts

Water cycle, water flow, properties of water, weather

Content Related Words

Evaporation, condensation, erosion, cascade, palisades, mist, storm front, thunderhead

Activities

1. *Water Dance* is an example of a "circle" book. It begins at a particular point, progresses, and finishes where it began. To acquaint the children with "circle" books, have them read *If You Give a Mouse a Cookie*, *If You Give a Moose a Muffin*, or *If You Give a Pig a Pancake* by Laura Numeroff.

2. Have the children make a bulletin board to serve as a backdrop for the activities in this unit. They should use pictures of water in its various forms (e.g., Niagara Falls, the Great Lakes, a morning fog in the forest, cloud formations). Calendar art is especially helpful for this topic. Ask a library media specialist to provide assistance.

3. Children may want to build their background knowledge of this topic by searching the Internet. Use the keywords *water cycle* to access information.

4. Lakes are especially important to the water cycle because they provide huge quantities of water for evaporation. On a map of their state, have children locate the larger lakes. What are the largest lakes in the United States? On a map of the desert Southwest, have children find the label *dry lake*. What do they think this means? Is the amount of rain in a given area dependent on the size of the lakes in that state?

47

5. In the water cycle (fig. 6.1), water evaporates from lakes and oceans; this water vapor becomes clouds and falls as rain. Ask children how the process of evaporation is speeded in nature. How do people speed evaporation in their own lives (e.g., to dry laundry, to dry hair)? NOTE: Any source of dry heat will speed evaporation, as will a dry wind.

6. Have the children examine a map such as the map in fig. 6.2. After they are familiar with it, examine one of their local area. What rivers, lakes, ponds, and reservoirs do they recognize by name or because they have visited these places? Were these bodies of water influential in settling the area? Are these bodies of water used as direct sources of drinking water? Are the water sources used for special purposes (e.g., recreation)?

7. Precipitation statistics include rainfall and snowfall. Together, they represent the amount of total rainfall for a given period of time. Using the data listed below, have the children make a line graph (fig. 6.3) to indicate the average amount of rainfall per month for one year in Pittsburgh, Pennsylvania. Based on this graph, write math problems for the children to solve (e.g., What is the average amount of rainfall per year? What is the wettest season of the year? What is the driest season of the year?). The data below is based on a 30-year average of the rainfall amount for each month. Ask children why an average is used instead of specific data for a particular year. Have children compare these numbers to those of the present year. Can they predict the amount of rainfall that will fall as the year progresses? Are the present year's numbers higher or lower than the averages? Obtain statistics for the local area and repeat these activities. NOTE: AccuWeather, a national weather service, can be accessed on the Internet at www.accuwx.com (accessed Sept. 22, 1998) or contacted at 385 Science Park Rd., State College, PA 16803, phone (814) 237-0309.

Monthly Precipitation Averages for One Year
Pittsburgh, Pennsylvania Airport

January	2.5"
February	2.4"
March	3.4"
April	3.2"
May	4.0"
June	3.7"
July	3.8"
August	3.2"
September	3.0"
October	2.4"
November	1.9"
December	1.9"

Text continues on page 52.

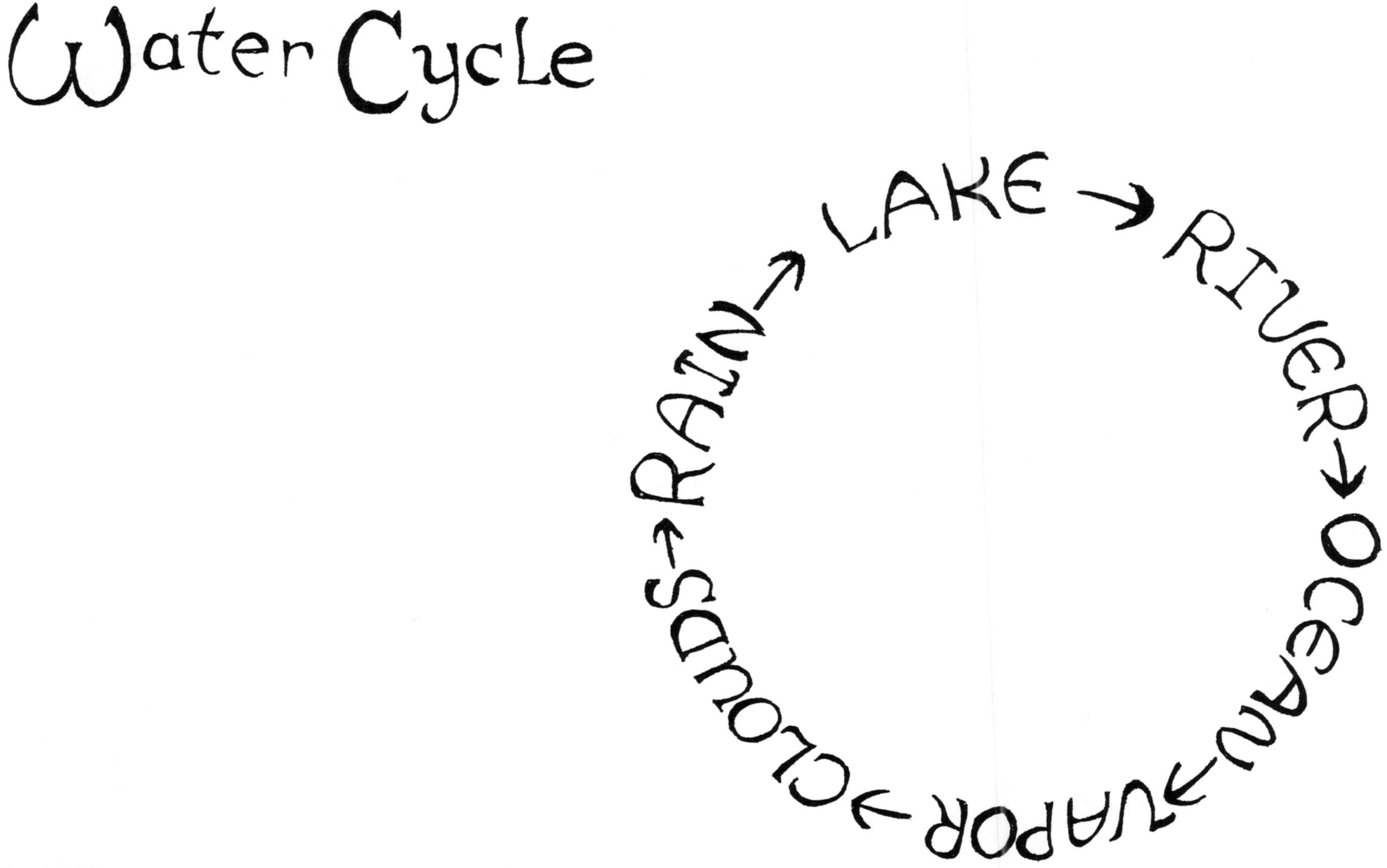

Water Cycle

RIVER → OCEAN → VAPOR → CLOUDS → RAIN → LAKE → RIVER

Fig. 6.1. The water cycle.

From *Exploring the Environment Through Children's Literature.* © 1999 Butzow and Butzow. Teacher Ideas Press. (800) 237-6124.

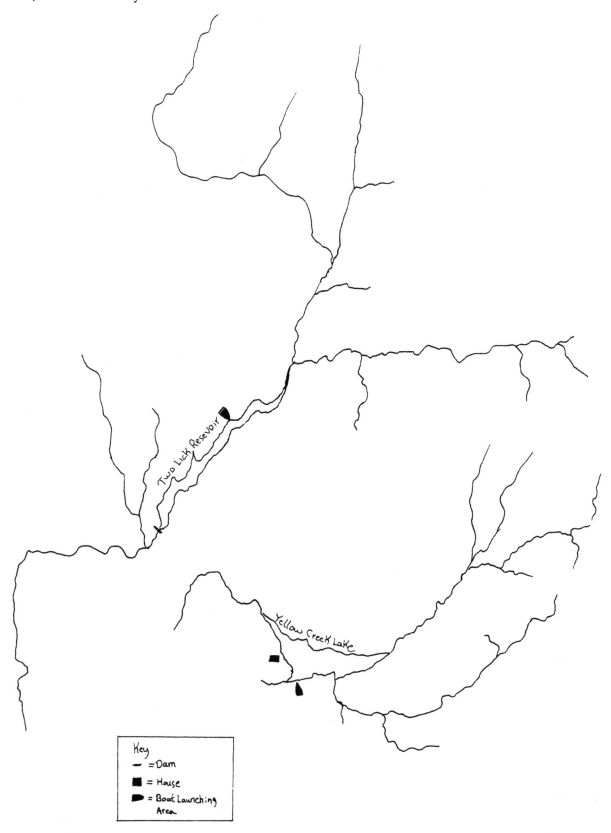

Fig. 6.2. Two water systems.

From *Exploring the Environment Through Children's Literature.* © 1999 Butzow and Butzow. Teacher Ideas Press. (800) 237-6124.

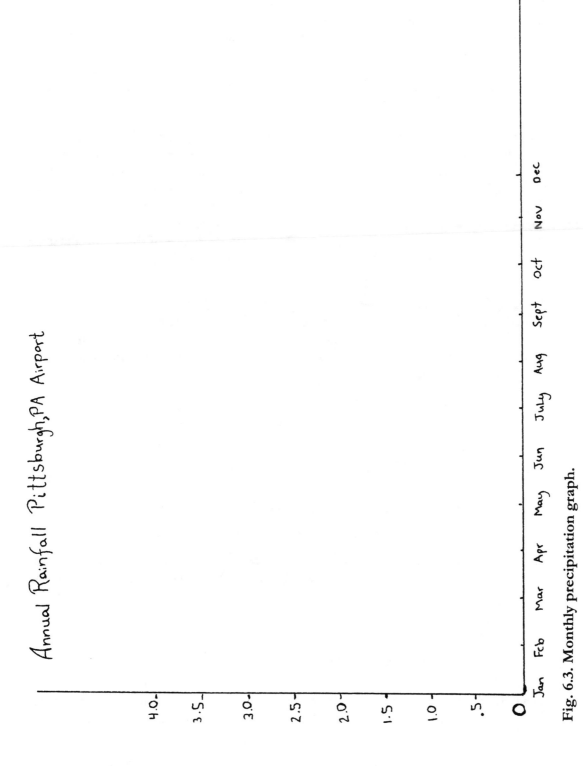

Annual Rainfall Pittsburgh, PA Airport

4.0
3.5
3.0
2.5
2.0
1.5
1.0
.5
0

Jan Feb Mar Apr May Jun July Aug Sept Oct Nov Dec

Fig. 6.3. Monthly precipitation graph.

From *Exploring the Environment Through Children's Literature.* © 1999 Butzow and Butzow. Teacher Ideas Press. (800) 237-6124.

8. The amount of rainfall that falls in a given geographic area greatly influences the weather and climate of that area. Using a weather or precipitation map from the library media center, have children study other cities of the United States (e.g., Portsmouth, New Hampshire; Seattle, Washington; Yuma, Arizona; Charlotte, North Carolina) and deduce how life there would be different from life in their city. Have children write out these comparisons or make a chart to show the differences. NOTE: The Internet can be a helpful source of information for this task.

9. At one time or another, most children probably think that thunder and lightning are produced in some magical way. As a creative writing exercise, have the children write fairy tales or myths to explain the existence of thunder and lightning. They may want to interview younger children, such as kindergartners, to obtain "research data" for this topic. Titles of the compositions might include "How the Thunder Got Its Voice," "Why the Lightning Flashes in the Sky," and "Flash, Bang, Kaboom!" NOTE: Lightning is a discharge of atmospheric electricity that overcomes the resistance of the air, producing a visible flash in the sky. The lightning discharge expands the air, producing a compression wave, the sound of which is thunder.

10. Dancing is a rhythmic movement. Each of the stages of the water cycle might be represented by a different dance or rhythmic movement. Divide the class into groups and assign each a stage of the cycle. They should create a rhythm that personifies the water at that stage. The children might want to expand their rhythm to create a pantomime that tells a story about their portion of the water cycle.

11. These nursery rhymes are reminiscent of the water cycle:

> Rain, rain, go away,
> Come again some other day,
> Little Johnny wants to play.
>
> It's raining , it's pouring, the old man is snoring,
> Went to bed and bumped his head, and wouldn't get up 'til morning.

Have the children write their own rhymes about rain or weather in general.

12. Have children write other verse about the water cycle. They might want to use a specific pattern, such as the limerick or cinquain, or use a rap format. The following example is a cinquain:

> The Mist
> Foggy, hazy
> Lifting, rising, floating
> Blotted out by sunlight streaming,
> All clear

Have the children write their nursery rhymes and verse from the previous activities on cutouts of large waterdrops (fig. 6.4). Hang these in the classroom to produce a rainfall display.

13. Have children view the famous scene from the movie *Singing in the Rain* in which Gene Kelly dances in the rain, complete with an open umbrella and soggy clothes. Ask them how the rain contributes to the presentation of this dance. How does the rain make the scene more humorous? What part does the musical score play in constructing this scene? Ask the children if they feel sorry for Mr. Kelly because he is getting wet.

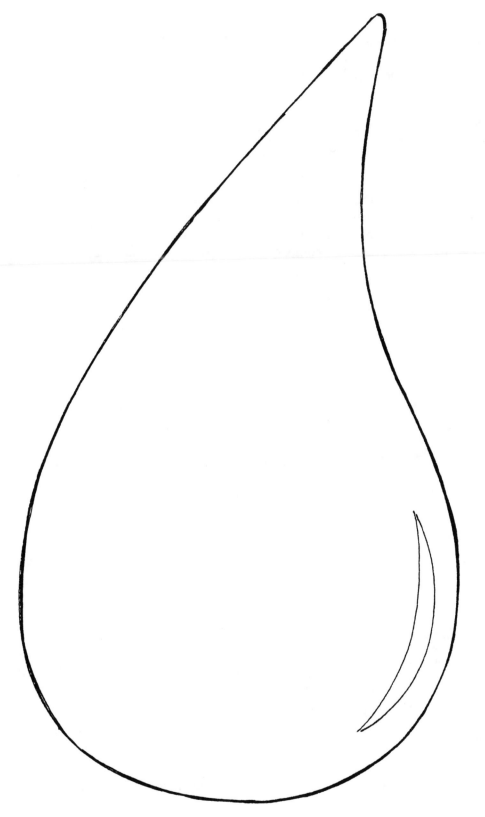

Fig. 6.4. Waterdrop writing form.

From *Exploring the Environment Through Children's Literature.* © 1999 Butzow and Butzow. Teacher Ideas Press. (800) 237-6124.

14. Any of the dance activities from the unit on *Earthdance* (Chapter 5) can be applied to this unit on *Water Dance*. Have children relate the stages of the water cycle to the other Earth rhythms they studied in the unit on *Earthdance*. How does the rhythm of the water cycle relate to the rhythms that people follow?

15. Children might be interested in hearing the story *The Sun, the Wind and the Rain* by Lisa Westerberg Peters, which portrays how water (as well as the sun and the wind) affects Earth. Another story about how water affects Earth, adversely, is *Flood* by Mary Calhoun (see Chapter 9).

16. Other stories by Thomas Locker include *Where the River Begins* and *The Boy Who Held Back the Sea*. Among the stories he has illustrated are *Catskill Eagle* by Herman Melville and *The Ice Horse* by Candace Christiansen. Some people think that his drawings are very similar to those of the Hudson River school of painters. Have children use the library media center to research these artists and compare their works to Locker's.

17. Word Scramble/Word Search—*Water Dance*
    Unscramble the "water" words below and match them with the clues.

niar	tims
teamsr	scolud
flaretawl	troms torfn
keal	deadherunth
revir	morst
esa	warinob

CLUES

a. Vaporlike water

b. Cascading waters

c. An ocean

d. A landlocked body of water

e. Falling droplets of water

f. A small amount of flowing water

g. Storm cloud producing thunder

h. A mass of vapor in the sky; patterns of moisture

i. Colors formed by sunlight reflecting off rain

j. Strong wind, with rain or snow

k. A large stream

l. An abrupt change in air pressure, usually accompanied by wind and rain

From *Exploring the Environment Through Children's Literature*. © 1999 Butzow and Butzow. Teacher Ideas Press. (800) 237-6124.

WORDS USED

clouds	sea
lake	storm
mist	storm front
rain	stream
rainbow	thunderhead
river	waterfall

The unscrambled words are hidden in this word search—horizontally, vertically, and diagonally, forwards and backwards.

A T N O R F M R O T S C E G
H J M P W O B N I A R S W Z
A F H N B O Z W C W V D R S
T E A C B N I A R F D E Q M
R N I L Q J W T X K E Y S I
I S Z O D Q N E O B K S T P
V T H U N D E R H E A D O I
E R R D S C B F T A L U R R
R E V S G S E A W P X O M Y
Z A D F V I D L H O V L L M
F M I S T N D L E I R C A N
A R O I C H I B R J K D I E

Fig. 6.5. Word Search—*Water Dance*.

From *Exploring the Environment Through Children's Literature.* © 1999 Butzow and Butzow. Teacher Ideas Press. (800) 237-6124.

Related Books and References

Calhoun, Mary. *Flood.* New York: Morrow Junior Books, 1997.

Christiansen, Candace. *The Ice Horse.* Illustrated by Thomas Locker. New York: Dial Books, 1993.

Koziel, Kathleen. "The Water Cycler." *Science and Children* 32, no. 1 (September 1994): 42–43.

Locker, Thomas. *The Boy Who Held Back the Sea.* New York: Dial Books, 1986.

———. *Where the River Begins.* New York: Dial Books, 1987.

Melville, Herman. *Catskill Eagle.* Illustrated by Thomas Locker. New York: Philomel, 1991.

Mitchell, John. "Our Polluted Runoff." *National Geographic* 189, no. 2 (February 1996): 106–25.

Monroe, Martha. "The All New Water Review." *Science and Children* 27, no. 4 (January 1990): 33–35.

Numeroff, Laura. *If You Give a Moose a Muffin.* New York: Harper Children's Books, 1991.

———. *If You Give a Mouse a Cookie.* New York: Harper Children's Books, 1991.

———. *If You Give a Pig a Pancake.* New York: Harper Children's Books, 1998.

Peters, Lisa Westerberg. *The Sun, the Wind and the Rain.* New York: Henry Holt, 1988.

Ryder, Joanne. *Earthdance.* New York: Henry Holt, 1996.

Singing in the Rain. Produced by Arthur Freed. Directed by Gene Kelly and Stanley Donen. MGM Home Video, 1951. Videocassette #M600185.

Chapter 7

Watershed Management

Letting Swift River Go

by Jane Yolen
Boston: Little, Brown, 1992

Summary

When the Windsor Dam was built to form the Quabbin Reservoir, the people in the valley near the Swift River had to move to new homes. Sally Jane remembered the old days but realized that life would never be the same, and so she heeded her mother's advice: "You have to let them go."

Science and Content Related Concepts

Water resources, watersheds, sources of water, regional planning, community change, displacement of people

Content Related Words

Dams, flooding, reservoir, technology, ghost towns, "woodpeckers," caissons, topographical

Activities

1. To prepare for this story, teachers can activate the children's imaginations by reading the Author's Note at the beginning of the book. Have the children set a purpose for reading the selection and for predicting the events of the story.

2. On a map of Massachusetts, have children locate the Quabbin Reservoir and Windsor Dam. What are the names of the small towns that surround the reservoir and the dam? How far away are Boston and the more populated areas of the state? NOTE: A Massachusetts highway map should provide all the details needed for this activity.

3. In an encyclopedia, almanac, or other reference work, have children look up the word *reservoir*. Have them explore the reasons for building reservoirs, the kinds of reservoirs, and the specific problems that must be overcome to build them. Have children name and locate the largest dams/reservoirs in the United States.

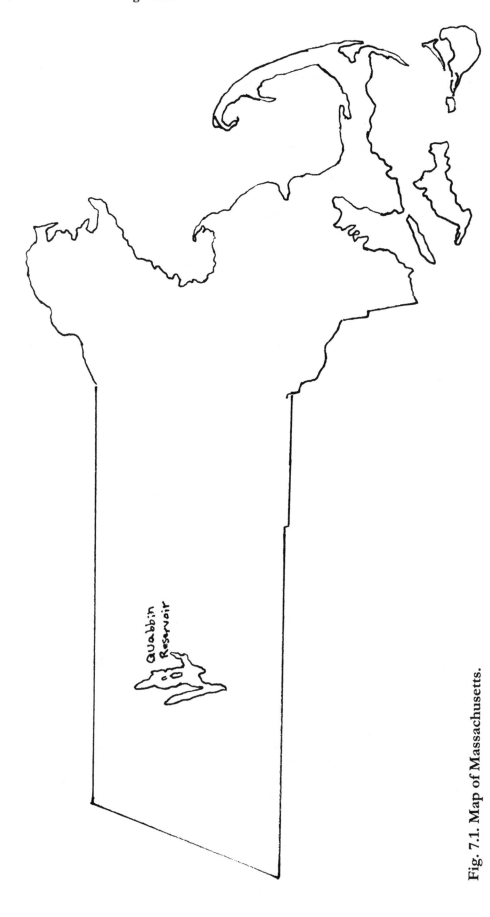

Quabbin Reservoir

Fig. 7.1. Map of Massachusetts.

From *Exploring the Environment Through Children's Literature.* © 1999 Butzow and Butzow. Teacher Ideas Press. (800) 237-6124.

4. Providing water for big cities is a major reason for building dams. Have children identify the water needs of people in such cities (e.g., industrial input, residential use). Have them make a chart for categorizing water needs.

5. A watershed is an area of land drained by a particular stream or river. In this book, the entire watershed area of the Swift River was flooded. Have the children research where streams or rivers in their community flow. What pathways do these streams follow as they become rivers and eventually empty into the ocean?

6. Topographical maps show the shapes or contours of the land. The land is measured in distance above sea level, not distance above the nearest flat land. Using the topographical map shown in figure 7.2, have children shade in the area that would be flooded if a dam were built across Brush Creek and flooded to an elevation of 350 feet above sea level. This means that everything below 350 feet above sea level would be flooded. On the map are houses, a church, and barns. Which of these buildings will be under water if the dam floods at an altitude of 350 feet above sea level? This exercise can be repeated for other elevations. How would flooding these elevations change the area around Brush Creek?

7. Have the class imagine that they are residents of an area that is to be flooded because of the construction of a reservoir. To simulate this scenario, select six children to play members of the town council who are in favor of the new dam. Select six children to play members of the town council who are opposed to the new dam. The rest of the class will play townspeople with various opinions to voice. Have the children research their positions before debating the issue and bringing a vote to closure. The debate should be conducted according to proper rules of order.

8. If a town were to be covered by water, townspeople might assemble a collection of nonperishable items representative of the school, the community, and the environment. Ask children what items might be used to meaningfully represent their town and surrounding areas. Have them design and make a small museum or display case to hold these treasures that represent the children's home.

9. Have the children imagine that their houses are to be flooded by the waters of a new reservoir. If possible, give each child a disposable camera with 24 exposures of film. Have them list 24 items (or events) from their home and community that they would photograph if this were the only means of "keeping" them. Photos can be used as bulletin board displays or put into an album for each child. If it is not possible to have the children take pictures, have the children discuss and select 24 pictures that could be photographed by an adult and used for a bulletin board display.

10. To supplement the above scenario, have the children keep a journal of their last days at home. What emotions do they experience as their town slowly disappears and they move to a new location? Children should also list the personal items they would take with them.

11. During a flooding of a residential area as described in *Letting Swift River Go*, would it be possible to move some buildings to a new town? Who would decide which buildings would be moved? What criteria would be used in making this decision? Invite a speaker who knows about moving houses to share with the class background information for this topic. Have the children prepare questions for the speaker (e.g., What kinds of machines are used to lift the buildings? How is the new site prepared? How is a house placed onto a new foundation?).

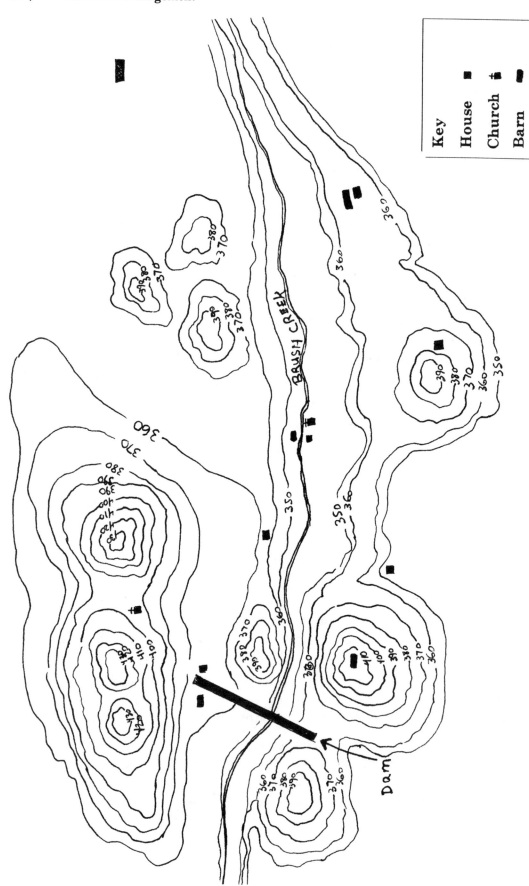

Fig. 7.2. Topographical map.

From *Exploring the Environment Through Children's Literature.* © 1999 Butzow and Butzow. Teacher Ideas Press. (800) 237-6124.

12. Older citizens such as grandparents and nursing-home residents are a helpful resource of information about the effects of natural or purposeful flooding of an area. Have class members interview older persons to ascertain the effects of natural flooding or reservoir projects on the community in past years. How did the natural flooding or construction of the reservoir affect the people in that area? Have these effects continued through generations to affect the children's lives today? NOTE: If the children do not live in an area where flooding occurs, have them use references in the library media center to research places such as Hoover Dam and Lake Mead. Also refer to Chapter 9 for the unit on *Flood* by Mary Calhoun.

13. Are there photos and/or newspaper accounts of floods in the community at a local historical society, library, or newspaper office? If so, copy these photo articles for use in a class discussion and as a wall display.

14. In the story, the children picnic on Grampa Will's grave. The black stone was quite warm. Have the class investigate this phenomenon by placing items of various colors in direct sunlight. Which items best absorb heat from the sun? Which absorb little or no heat? What can the children infer about colors of clothing, automobiles, and so on?

15. To show how flood water might cover a town, have the children build a small model town in a basin or tub using clay or Play Doh. Plastic models of buildings will be useful but should be secured in the clay so that they do not float. There should be various elevations in the town. When the town is complete, slowly pour water into the basin or tub. Which areas are flooded first? Which are flooded last? How would flooding change the terrain of the area? How would this affect the persons who have moved to higher ground?

16. In the story, fishing was an important pastime, both before the dam was built and afterwards. What game fish live in the local area? How are different species of fish distinguished from one another? What rules govern the licensing of persons who want to fish in the area? Invite someone who is well known for their fishing abilities to discuss with the class local game fish and fishing.

Fig. 7.3. Submerged town.

17. The U.S. Army Corps of Engineers maintains dams and waterways in many states. Using the Internet as a resource, have children determine if there is a U.S. Army Corps of Engineers installation near their community. If so, arrange a field trip to the site or invite a member of the corps to speak to the class. While using the Internet, have children access the Corps of Engineers GORP—Great Outdoor Recreation Pages. Have the children use a state highway map to locate and mark the sites nearest their community. The Corps of Engineers can be reached at http://www.usace.army. mil (accessed Sept. 22, 1998).

18. *Letting Swift River Go* is a true story. There are two museums dedicated to the towns that were flooded by Quabbin Reservoir—Dana, Prescott, Enfield, and Greenwich. Children may want to contact these two museums:

    The Swift River Valley Historical Society, Inc.
    40 Elm Street
    New Salem, MA 01355
    508-544-6882

    Belchertown Historical Association
    Box 1211, Maple Street
    Belchertown, MA 01007
    413-323-6573

19. Math Puzzle—*Letting Swift River Go*
    Solve the following arithmetic problems, then match the answers to the alphabet chart to decode the message.

A	B	C	D	E	F	G	H	I	J	K	L	M
1	2	3	4	5	6	7	8	9	10	11	12	13

N	O	P	Q	R	S	T	U	V	W	X	Y	Z
14	15	16	17	18	19	20	21	22	23	24	25	26

____   ____   ____   ____   ____   ____   ____

5x5   3x5   11+10   4x2   1+0   12+10   4+1

____   ____   ____   ____   ____

14+6   12+3   7+5   3+2   18+2

____   ____   ____   ____   ____   ____

4x5   2x4   3+2   7+6   10-3   12+3

From *Exploring the Environment Through Children's Literature.* © 1999 Butzow and Butzow. Teacher Ideas Press. (800) 237-6124.

Related Books and References

Gannaway, Susan P. "Watching the Watershed." *Science and Children* 33, no. 4 (January 1996): 16–18.

Mattingly, Rosanna L. "Don't Change That Channel!" *The Science Teacher* 60, no. 3 (March 1993): 24–31.

Chapter 8

Effects of Industry on Water

A River Ran Wild

by Lynne Cherry
San Diego, CA: Harcourt Brace Jovanovich, 1992

Summary

It was the land of the Nash-a-way—the river with the Pebbled Bottom. This was the home of the Indians, but one day the settlers came with a way of life that did not match that of the Indians. In time, the ways of both groups would be changed by the industrialization of the area and the pollution of the Nashua River. Through the intervention of countless concerned persons, the Nashua once more became the river with the Pebbled Bottom—the river that ran wild. NOTE: During the time this story takes place, *Indian* was the proper term of address, as opposed to the term *Native American* used today. *Indian* will be used throughout this unit.

Science and Content Related Concepts

Natural resources, replenishment of resources, environment, barter economy, manufacturing, Industrial Revolution, water clarity, multiculturalism

Content Related Words

Nash-a-way (Nashua), settlers, generations, migration, trading post, paper pulp, millponds, technology, machine, environmental resources, progress, dams, inventions, Industrial Revolution

Activities

1. To exemplify the concept of historical time, knot a ball of string every 10 inches. Each 10-inch segment is equivalent to 10 years—approximately as long as the children have been alive, or one child's lifetime. Use the string to designate the dates listed on the inside cover of the book (e.g., 1830—The Indian Removal Act). Ask the children how many "lifetimes" ago these events occurred. What other events might be added to the timeline (e.g., the Revolutionary War, Abraham Lincoln's assassination, the first human-operated rocket in space)? NOTE: To mark events on the timeline, write the event on a small card and then hang it on the timeline with a paper clip pierced through the card.

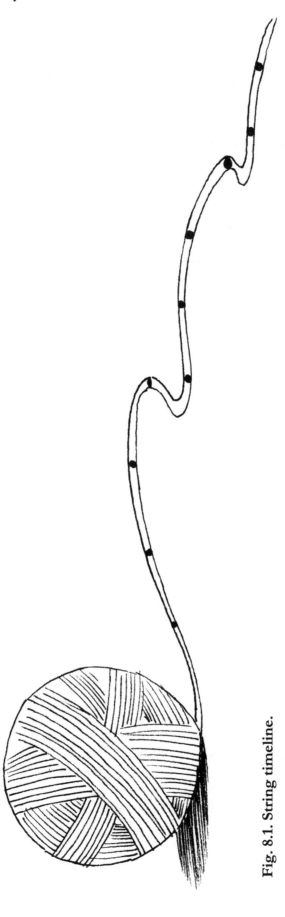

Fig. 8.1. String timeline.

From *Exploring the Environment Through Children's Literature.* © 1999 Butzow and Butzow. Teacher Ideas Press. (800) 237-6124.

2. Before the European colonization of the Massachusetts/New Hampshire area, what environment would have been found in the area of the Nash-a-way river? To learn more about the environment at the time of the first white settlers, have children check encyclopedias or reference books for information about the settling of New England.

3. The Industrial Revolution began exerting an influence on the United States during the 1700s. Was their local town a part of this change from an agrarian society to an industrial one? If so, have children research what industries were involved. Was there a succession of different kinds of industries? What industries exist now? If there are no industries in the town, have children research the industries of an appropriate nearby city. The library media specialist should have information on these topics.

4. Have a "Technology Fair" in which simple hand tools are displayed. Have children research how these items were manufactured. What are or were the purposes of these tools? Have they been replaced by technologically advanced items (e.g., a curling iron that was heated in a flame before applying it to the hair, compared to an electric curling iron)? NOTE: Old hand tools can often be found at garage sales and auctions, as well as in friends' basements.

5. Have children design a "new" mechanical tool that can be used for a specific, demonstrable purpose. They should designate an appropriate name for this item and write a brief summary of how it works.

6. The Nashua River became polluted as a result of factories dumping waste into the water. This pollution causes the water to become cloudy. The simplest measure of water clarity is obtained by using a Secchi disk (fig. 8.2). This implement is lowered into the water until the disk can no longer be seen. Using the string attached to the disk, the distance at which the disk can no longer be seen is measured. Have children use a Secchi disk to take several readings in various parts of a nearby stream and then average the results. NOTE: Swiftly flowing water will invalidate the measurements; work at a calm section of the stream. Children working in the water should be paired together and supervised by an adult; or, the activity can be done by an adult and the results shared with the children.

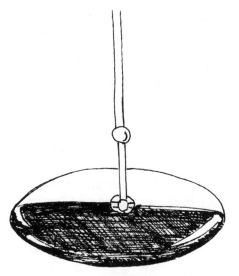

Fig. 8.2. Secchi disk.

7. If the school is located near a factory that will allow children to visit, ask factory officials to arrange a guided tour for the class. How old is the factory? What products are manufactured there? What regulations must be followed when disposing of waste products? How does the factory help contribute to a clean environment? What environmental problems must still be solved?

8. The Nashua River was nearly destroyed because of the waste and other pollutants dumped into it. Today, such dumping is illegal, and water must be treated before it can reenter the environment. Visit a local sewage disposal plant with the class. What impurities exist in the town's water supply? How is the water purified? What are the criteria for judging whether water is clean enough to use? Do any wastes result from the purification procedure? Who polices this water treatment plant to ensure that all pertinent laws are upheld?

9. Water contamination is a common problem, as is air pollution. To be better informed about the local community, save articles from newspapers, magazines, and other publications that describe local environmental issues. What are these concerns? What is being done about them? Are there actions that continue to contribute to the problems? Have the children write a proposal suggesting what actions should be taken to help solve these problems. Have the children make posters using these clippings and writings, and share the posters with the entire school.

10. Have children study a 10-mile section of a nearby river. Collect information about the river by taking the class on a field trip to the river. Take photographs of the area; write descriptions; interview people who live or work along the river; take water samples. Back in the classroom, make a large bulletin board display of this section of the river. On the display, post the photos and writings about the river. Label industrial products of the area, residential areas, and any obstructions on the river. After gathering all this information, have the children answer these questions: Is the river polluted to the point that it threatens the quality of life in the area? Is the water clean and usable to the nearby inhabitants? Is the river in the process of being cleaned up? If so, who is in charge of the project? What kind of work is being done? What is the anticipated date of returning the river to its former status? What other purposes does the river serve (e.g., recreation)?

11. In most states and communities in the United States, wastewater from industry and private homes must meet particular standards of purity before it can reenter the environment. These standards differ from community to community. Generally, they specify that the treated wastewater be of fairly high quality. Invite an officer from the Environmental Protection Agency, or a local waterworks official, to visit the class and explain the standards that treated wastewater must meet.

12. A lady named Marian was important to the story of the Nashua River. She made many speeches to help clean up the pollution in this area. Have the children write a speech stating what they think she would say to those who gathered to listen to her. Children should edit their speeches and then recite them for the class. Having children work in small groups may be more effective in allowing everyone a chance to speak.

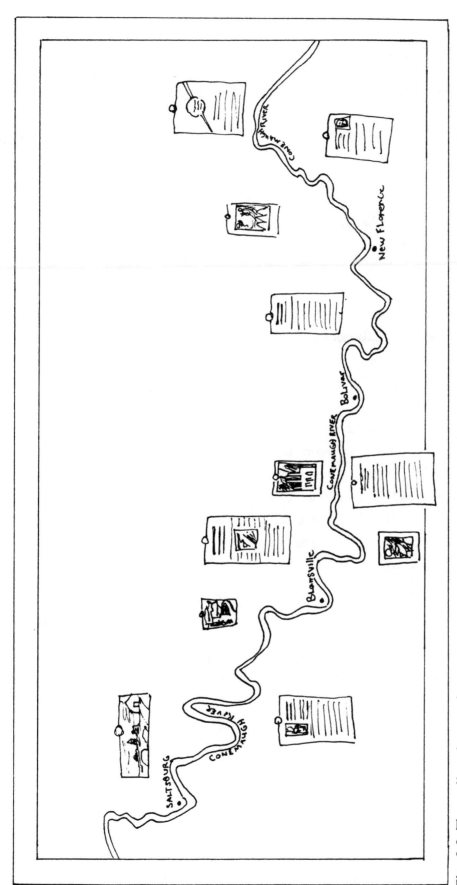

Fig. 8.3. Ten miles along a river.

From *Exploring the Environment Through Children's Literature.* © 1999 Butzow and Butzow. Teacher Ideas Press. (800) 237-6124.

13. Using the Internet or another recent source, have children find out about modern day Nashua. Use the following Web site: http://www.nashuachamber.com/Region/nashua.htm (accessed Sept. 22, 1998) or use the key words *Nashua, New Hampshire*. Have the children find information on such topics as history, industries, and economy.

14. Word Search—*A River Ran Wild*

Words used in the story *A River Ran Wild* are hidden in this word search horizontally and vertically, forwards and backwards. First, match the words to the clues.

CLUES

a. A mountain near the Nash-a-way (two words)

b. Dirty air and water

c. A lady who spoke against polluting the river

d. An Indian crop

e. Today's name for the river in the story

f. An animal that builds dams in the river

g. Fish that live in clean waters

h. A place for exchanging goods (two words)

i. Settlers brought these to trade with the Indians

j. The Nash-a-way was known as the river with the _____ _____

k. Machines were first used during the _____ Revolution

l. This animal is related to the deer

m. An object that helps one do work more easily

n. The leader of the Indians in the story (two words)

o. They were used for thatching roofs on homes

p. To go, uninvited, on someone else's property

WORDS USED

beaver	Industrial	moose	pollution
cattails	machine	Mt. Wachusett	salmon
Chief Weeawa	Marian	Nashua	trading post
corn	mirrors	Pebbled Bottom	trespass

From *Exploring the Environment Through Children's Literature*. © 1999 Butzow and Butzow. Teacher Ideas Press. (800) 237-6124.

Fig. 8.4. Word Search—*A River Ran Wild.*

Related Books and References

Cole, Joanna. *The Magic Schoolbus at the Waterworks.* New York: Scholastic, 1986.

George, Arnold. "Testing the Water." *Science and Children* 29, no. 6 (March 1992): 32–33.

Green, Tom. "Watershed Science." *The Science Teacher* 63, no. 1 (January 1996): 34–36.

Rivera, Deborah B., and Mary M. Banbury. "Conserving Water: Every Drop Makes a Difference." *Science Scope* 17, no. 8 (May 1994): 15–17.

Vandas, Steve. "Woodlands: Water, Wildlife, Plants, and People." *Science and Children* 30, no. 1 (September 1992): 39–41.

Vandas, Steve, and Nancy J. Crotin. "Hazardous Waste: Cleanup and Prevention." *Science and Children* 33, no. 7 (April 1996): 23–24+.

From *Exploring the Environment Through Children's Literature.* © 1999 Butzow and Butzow. Teacher Ideas Press. (800) 237-6124.

Chapter 9

Natural Disaster

Flood

by Mary Calhoun
New York: Morrow Junior Books, 1997

Summary

Rivers can become raging torrents driving people from their homes and leaving a path of destruction. After the flood waters recede, it is necessary to decide whether to rebuild homes and businesses or relocate them on higher ground.

Science and Content Related Concepts

Floods, flood preparedness, low-pressure areas

Content Related Words

Levee, sandbag, upstream, overflow, johnboat, floodstage, crest, watershed

Activities

1. Have the children work with their parents or other older persons to make a "Disaster Preparation Checklist." This should include evacuation plans for leaving the house or apartment, a meeting place for the family after the evacuation, supplies to take and designation of who would take them, any particular needs that members of the family might have (e.g., diapers, medication for high blood pressure), and so on. Have the class discuss their checklists and compile a composite list to produce and distribute to parents. Have the class illustrate the checklist with appropriate scenes.

2. The American Red Cross produces pamphlets about disaster preparedness, as well as about each type of natural disaster (e.g., hurricanes, tornadoes, winter storms). Obtain these pamphlets and have children compare them to the checklist they produced in the previous activity.

3. Have children research the topic of evacuation and natural disasters using the Internet. The keywords *civil defense* and *flood preparedness* will access many sources for discussion.

4. In areas where there is a history of flooding, plans must be made to aid the citizens of the area when a flood is imminent. Have the children discuss relevant topics, such as criteria for the selection of emergency shelters, provisions for obtaining blankets and clothing, sources of food and medical supplies, use of generators to produce electricity, maintenance of telephone lines, sandbagging, evacuation, and so on. Who would be in charge of these operations? What persons would be needed to fulfill these jobs? Are they paid officials or volunteers? How would the emotional needs of the citizens be met, as well as the physical needs?

5. Providing emergency shelter and food is of utmost importance at the time of any natural disaster. Have the children list places in their town that could serve as emergency shelters. Check with town officials to determine if there are designated shelters and, if so, where they are located. What provisions should be made for food service?

6. Many volunteers are needed to help at the time of a flood. Have the children prepare possible advertisements that could be placed on the Internet in time of need. This ad would seek help in all necessary areas, such a sandbagging, evacuating people, keeping utility services operating, collecting food and clothing, and so on. The advertisement should specify the location of the devastated area and detail the work areas to be maintained. Include the name and e-mail address of a contact person.

7. Have the children identify markers on their house that would indicate that flood waters had reached levels of three, six, and twelve feet. For each of these levels, have children list the most important items that would need to be saved from the rising waters. Children may want to compile their lists room by room, or they may want to consider just their own living area. NOTE: Flood waters are measured by recording the height of the water above ground level.

8. If there were little time to rescue household goods during a flood, what would be the most important items for each child to rescue? Have children make a collage showing the items they would rescue. Is there an overlap of particular items among the children? If so, have the children graph the results of a survey of items (e.g., stereo equipment and sports equipment might be listed by several children, while few may mention furniture).

9. Do any of the children have a canoe or a boat of some type in their garage? How could it be used to help the family or others in the neighborhood? Do the local police or other emergency organizations have boats to enable them to help citizens?

10. During a flood, some stores and services can remain open, if they are on high ground away from the flood waters, to assist the citizens of the community. Have children identify which stores and services in their town fit this description. How would people be able to determine which businesses remain open during a flood? Would people be able to reach them?

11. In the story, Sarajean's grandmother did not want to leave her home, even though the flood waters were swiftly rising. Why do some people seem oblivious to danger? Have children play the roles of workers such as the sheriff, the civil defense coordinator, town officials, volunteers of the American Red Cross, and so on. How would they convince people to leave their homes? Would they ever allow people to stay?

12. Have children compare the Lorton family, discussed in "The Great Flood of '93" by Alan Mairson in *National Geographic*, to Sarajean's family. What experiences did the two families share? How were their experiences different?

13. Using a map of the local area, have the children locate the streams and rivers that could possibly flood their area. Which waterways have a history of flooding? Which have rarely flooded? Local newspaper offices should have files of articles about past floods. Have the children photocopy pictures and articles to make a bulletin board display.

14. Another source of information about previous floods are people who have actually experienced them during their lifetime. Invite some of these persons to tell their stories to the class.

15. A detailed map of the Missouri-Mississippi River area appears in "The Great Flood of '93" by Alan Mairson in *National Geographic*. Have children write in the names of the Midwestern states that were affected by the high flood waters in 1993. Locate the rivers that overflowed their banks. Compare the maps to a landform map of the United States. Ask children what landform these states have in common. Ask a library media specialist to help children find other newspapers and magazines with articles about the flood of 1993. NOTE: States with counties eligible for federal disaster-area relief funds for this flood included Wisconsin, Minnesota, Illinois, Iowa, Missouri, Nebraska, Kansas, South Dakota, and North Dakota. Rivers that overflowed included the Mississippi, Missouri, Minnesota, Iowa, Raccoon, Big Sioux, Des Moines, and Illinois. Locate these states and rivers on a large map of the United States.

16. Why is it important for states and counties to be declared disaster areas, in the wake of great floods? Have a knowledgeable insurance agent or bank officer explain this situation to the class.

17. What are the effects of a flood? Have children list short-term effects, as well as long-term effects. How is cleanup handled? How is damage assessed? How do people obtain monetary assistance for rebuilding homes? What laws regulate construction on a floodplain? Are there ways to prevent future floods?

18. Devastating floods can cause much destruction to homes, yards, and businesses. Have the children conduct a decision-making exercise in which they must decide whether to rebuild a home or business on a floodplain, or move it to higher ground that is not likely to flood. Specific local businesses may be analyzed, as well as individual homes. Which choice would have a more positive effect on the environment?

19. Water that overflows its riverbanks scours into the earth. As the water recedes, sand deposits are left along the river. In figure 9.1, have children identify the sand deposits. What damage would these deposits cause? What would be the long-term effects of the sand?

20. Have children search the Internet using the keyword *levee*. What can they learn about a levee and its purpose? How are levees constructed? Who maintains them? Are there any levees in their town? What happens to levees if they are broken by flood waters?

21. How much rain and snow does the local area receive in a year? How much snow is equivalent to an inch of water? What is considered a "dry" year? What is a "wet" year? Obtain information from the U.S. Weather Bureau to answer these questions. How do town officials predict when waters may be rising too fast and will probably flood? Invite someone from a local weather bureau, or a town official, to discuss these issues with the class. NOTE: See also the unit on *Water Dance* (Chapter 6).

Text continues on page 78.

Sand Deposits

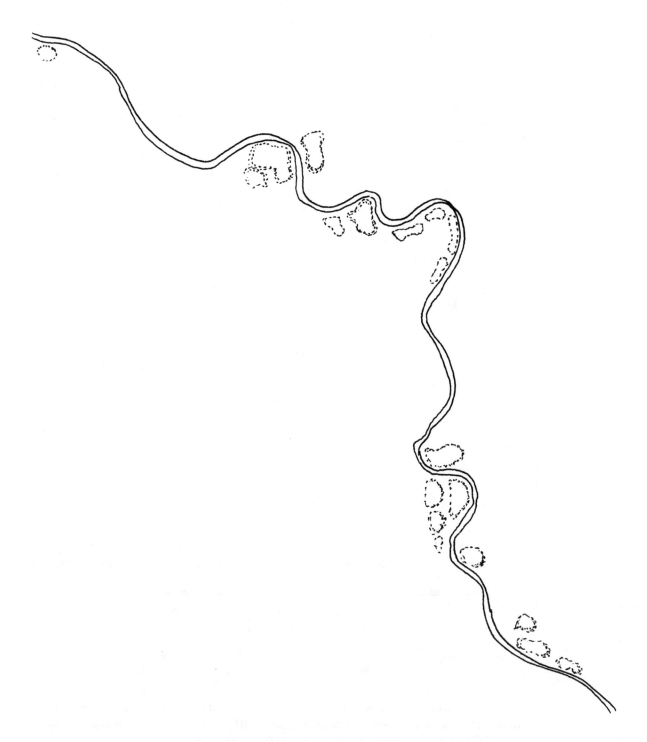

Fig. 9.1. Aftermath of river flooding.

From *Exploring the Environment Through Children's Literature.* © 1999 Butzow and Butzow. Teacher Ideas Press. (800) 237-6124.

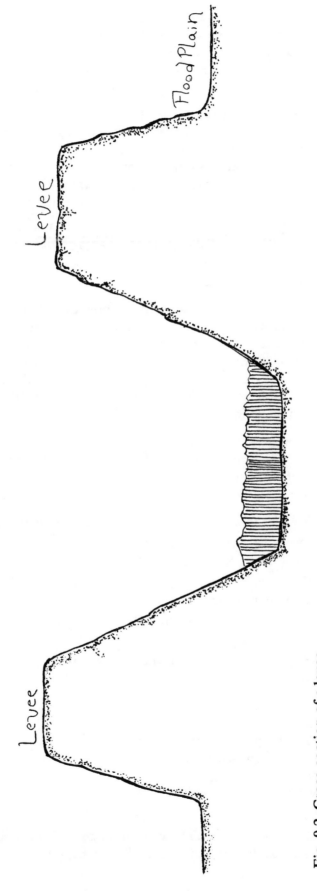

Fig. 9.2. Cross-section of a levee.

From *Exploring the Environment Through Children's Literature.* © 1999 Butzow and Butzow. Teacher Ideas Press. (800) 237-6124.

22. Most communities have been settled along the banks of rivers or streams. Why is this so? How have other areas flourished without being beside a water source? Have the children delve into some local history to research why and how their community was settled. Are there wetlands as well as streams in the area? If so, is there still a need for the waterway and these wetlands considering scientific and technological advances in industry and transportation?

23. People generally think of the flow of a river being straight. In reality, many rivers, such as the Mississippi, Missouri, Ohio, and Wabash, follow serpentine courses and even double back upon themselves. Sometimes the river changes course and the old path of the river becomes a lake. Have children study the map of the Mississippi River shown in figure 9.3. Can they determine where the course of the river has changed? Have them draw the old pathway of the river. How would they describe the way the river "meanders"?

24. Many rivers have been altered over the years by people. How is this done? What are the purposes of such changes? For example, the Kinzua Dam was built in western Pennsylvania to reduce flooding downstream in the city of Pittsburgh. Have children research this topic. Have people changed any local rivers?

25. Industrial production has often resulted in the pollution of water and the surrounding environment. Fortunately, many changes are being made and much of this pollution is being controlled. Rivers that were once polluted have become safe recreational areas. Have the children make triptychs showing the past, present, and future of the waterways and wetlands in their area. The future aspect of the work will be speculative and may include continued solving of pollution problems or fulfilling the needs of the people (e.g., the creation of marinas, a boardwalk).

26. Many adjectives and metaphors can be used to describe the sound of water (e.g., lapping waves, roaring torrents). Have the children think of adjectives and metaphors to describe various aspects of water, to use in some form of poetry. Children might enjoy writing a diamante, a seven-line poem that changes meaning in the middle:

> Line 1—A noun; the object to be described (a noun of opposite meaning will be line 7)
> Line 2—Two adjectives describing line 1
> Line 3—Three descriptive participles describing line 1 (words ending in *-ing* or *-ed*)
> Line 4—Four nouns: two synonyms for line 1, two synonyms for line 7 (which has the opposite meaning of line 1)
> Line 5—Three descriptive participles describing line 7
> Line 6—Two adjectives describing line 7
> Line 7—A noun with the opposite meaning of line 1

For example:

> Stream
> Leisurely, passive
> Bending, reflecting, journeying
> Rivulet, waterway—channel, current
> Roaring, raging, rampaging
> Wild, violent
> Torrent

NOTE: Children may find it easier to write lines 1 and 7 first and then work towards the middle. This is an excellent lesson for introducing the use of a thesaurus.

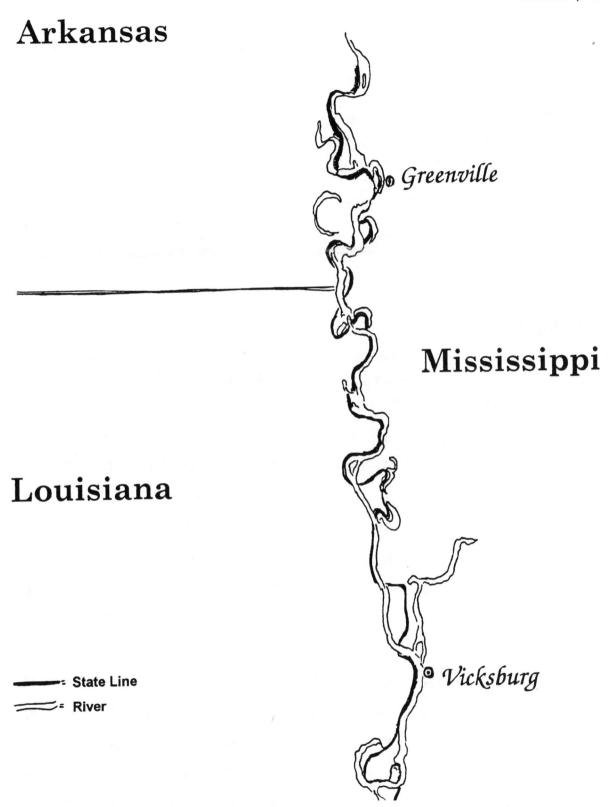

Arkansas

Louisiana

Greenville

Mississippi

Vicksburg

State Line

River

Fig. 9.3. Meanders in the Mississippi River.

From *Exploring the Environment Through Children's Literature.* © 1999 Butzow and Butzow. Teacher Ideas Press. (800) 237-6124.

27. Word Search—*Flood*

Words from the story *Flood* are hidden in this word search—horizontally, vertically, and diagonally, forwards and backwards.

CLUES

a. To go over the banks of a river

b. The greatest height to which the water rises

c. He or she warns people to leave their homes in an emergency

d. The direction from which the water flows

e. The longest river in the United States

f. A tributary leading to the Mississippi

g. To leave home and seek shelter

h. They are piled up to increase the height of the levee

i. He or she reports the weather news

j. Sarajean's family fled to safety in this

k. An earthen wall built to prevent floods

l. The point at which flooding begins

WORDS USED

evacuate
floodstage
forecaster

high water mark
johnboat
levee

Mississippi
Missouri
overflow

sandbags
sheriff
upstream

```
A  C  T  A  O  B  N  H  O  J  D  F  H
M  M  D  Q  R  O  V  E  R  F  L  O  W
F  I  C  A  R  M  A  R  I  N  O  P  Q
J  S  E  G  A  T  S  D  O  O  L  F  Z
A  S  D  F  A  G  B  Z  H  F  I  O  J
H  I  G  H  W  A  T  E  R  M  A  R  K
U  S  V  W  E  V  A  C  U  A  T  E  J
K  S  A  N  D  B  A  G  S  R  N  C  Q
M  I  S  S  O  U  R  I  Q  S  L  A  H
M  P  O  T  P  F  F  I  R  E  H  S  N
U  P  S  T  R  E  A  M  V  A  F  T  O
G  I  H  J  L  N  P  E  Q  S  P  E  U
A  F  M  B  N  P  E  C  O  E  D  R  T
```

Fig. 9.4. Word Search—*Flood*.

From *Exploring the Environment Through Children's Literature.* © 1999 Butzow and Butzow. Teacher Ideas Press. (800) 237-6124.

Related Books and References

Fisher, Marion, and Jack Lane. "Navigation: Traveling the Water Highways." *Science and Children* 32, no. 7 (April 1995): 16–18.

Locker, Thomas. *Water Dance.* San Diego, CA: Harcourt Brace Jovanovich, 1997.

Mairson, Alan. "Great Flood of '93." *National Geographic* 185, no. 1 (January 1994): 42–87.

Vandas, Steve. "Watersheds: Where We Live." *Science and Children* 34, no. 7 (April 1997): 28–30.

Part III

Environmental Impact

Chapter 10

Historical Patterns of Environmental Impact

Island Boy

by Barbara Cooney
New York: Viking Kestrel, 1988

Summary

When Pa and Ma brought their 12 children to Tibbetts Island, it was a new way of life for everyone. Self-sufficiency was the mode of existence. As years passed, their lives changed, but there was always their love for the island and their love for one another to see them through.

Science and Content Related Concepts

Landforms; marine environment; self-sufficiency; division of labor; cycle of life; family needs—food, shelter, clothing, education; interdependence of humanity and nature; adaptation to circumstances; death and dying

Content Related Words

Mainland, Tibbetts Island, schooner, Six Brothers, saltwater farms, rusticators, Astrakhan apple tree, weather, seasons, sea smoke, cormorants, eiders, gulls, terns, import, export

Activities

1. Schooners flew many navigational flags in addition to the United States flag. Have each child design and make a personal flag to "fly" during this unit.

2. *Island Boy* takes place in New England, probably in Maine. Have children locate Maine and the other five New England states on a large wall map of the United States. Which states were known for their seafaring ships during the age of the schooners, which lasted from approximately 1860 through 1920?

3. On the map of the eastern United States and the Caribbean Islands (fig. 10.1), have children locate the places to which Uncle Albion's ships sailed. Which products were exported from New England? Which were imported by people in towns such as Green Harbor?

Fig. 10.1. Map of the eastern United States and the Caribbean Islands.

From *Exploring the Environment Through Children's Literature.* © 1999 Butzow and Butzow. Teacher Ideas Press. (800) 237-6124.

4. Have the children make maps of Tibbetts Island using pictures and clues from the text (e.g., "It was Pa who felled the trees and cleared the north end of the island"). Children should include landforms and all objects that give evidence to the family living on the island (e.g., the barns, the well). The depiction of the island might also be done as a poster or diorama.

5. Have the children create a mural of Green Harbor showing the harbor and the sailing ships, as well as the townspeople. They should indicate the trades of the people: ship's captain, sailors, boat builders, sail makers, woodcutters, blacksmiths, farmers, housewives, teachers, wagon makers, hat makers, and any other appropriate occupations. Which occupations would the children choose to follow? What training would they need for this trade?

6. Three types of boats were commonly seen in Green Harbor—the schooner, the Friendship sloop, and the dinghy. Silhouettes of these three types of boats are included (fig. 10.2) for use in the children's mural of Green Harbor.

7. Sailors must know the direction in which they are sailing. The major directions are north, south, east, and west, as seen on the compass rose (fig. 10.3). It is common to designate the intermediate directions as northeast, southeast, southwest, and northwest. Have the children orient themselves to the directions in relationship to the classroom. Have them stand and play a Simon Says game using directions such as "Simon Says turn to the east," "Simon Says turn to the southwest," "Turn north," and so on. A player who acts upon a command not given by Simon must sit down. The last player standing is the winner.

8. Using the map and key shown in figure 10.4, have children solve the following sailing puzzles (e.g., Starting at Starbuck on Long Island and sailing almost due north for about 3¾ miles, where would you be?)
   Where will children be if they follow the compass directions below?
   a. Starting at Starbuck, sail northwest for 2 miles, then north for ¾ miles.
   b. Starting at Grays Head, sail southwest for 1 mile.
   c. Starting at Matthias Port, sail 2¾ miles south, then 1¾ miles west.
   d. Starting at Goat Island, sail 2 miles south, then 1 mile west.
   e. Starting at Gulf Port, sail 1½ miles south, then east for ¾ mile.
   f. Starting at Little Island, sail 2 miles northeast, then ½ mile north.

   Have children reverse their sailing skills. Name a starting point and a destination and ask them to provide directions for reaching that place:
   g. Grays Head to Gulf Port
   h. Bulls Head to Starbuck
   i. Gulf Port to Heart Island
   j. Gulf Port to Goat Island
   k. Matthias Port to Jonesport
   l. Bulls Head to Sharp Point

9. Have children perform the previous activity outdoors, using designated objects or places as starting points and destinations. Determine scale that will used (e.g., 1 step equals 1 mile). Design problems of both types presented in the previous activity.

Text continues on page 91.

Fig. 10.2. Silhouettes of schooner, sloop, and dinghy.

From *Exploring the Environment Through Children's Literature.* © 1999 Butzow and Butzow. Teacher Ideas Press. (800) 237-6124.

Fig. 10.3. Compass rose.

From *Exploring the Environment Through Children's Literature.* © 1999 Butzow and Butzow. Teacher Ideas Press. (800) 237-6124.

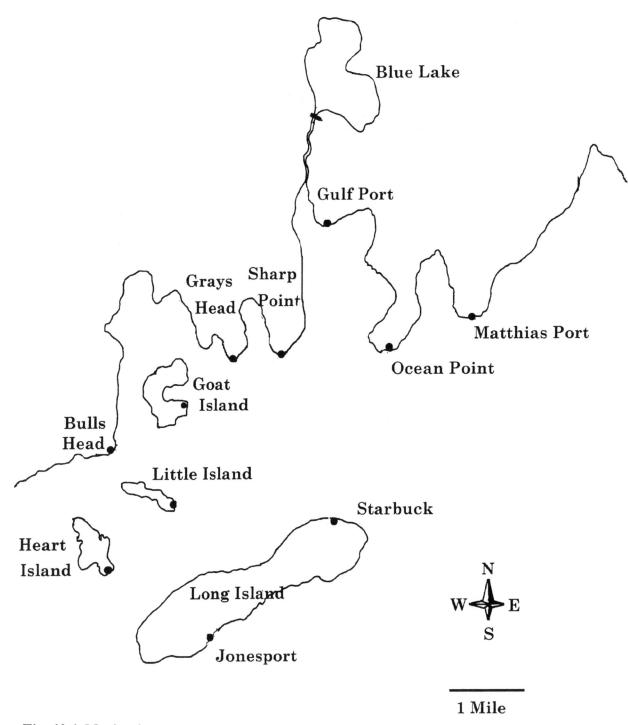

Fig. 10.4. Navigation map.

From *Exploring the Environment Through Children's Literature.* © 1999 Butzow and Butzow. Teacher Ideas Press. (800) 237-6124.

10. Discuss the division of labor between the men, women, and children on Tibbetts Island. Which jobs belonged to each group of people? Were there times when this division shifted and people acquired new jobs? How does this division of labor compare to today's division of labor?

11. *Self-sufficiency* is a term that relates to the ability of persons to provide for their own needs with little or no outside help. The Tibbetts family were nearly self-sufficient because they were able to exist with few store-bought goods and services. Have children compare the life of the Tibbetts family to life today regarding food, housing, energy use, schooling, clothing, and entertainment. Children may want to pantomime the two scenarios.

12. Help children plant a small vegetable garden in the classroom. Use fast-germinating seeds, such as peas, radishes, lettuce, and squash. Can you purchase hearty varieties that would be more suitable for the short growing season on Tibbetts Island? Styrofoam cups filled with potting soil or starter pellets should be used to grow the plants. Have children observe how long it takes for the seeds to germinate. If possible, have the children transplant the seedlings to large pots or a plot outdoors. If it is time for summer vacation, have a volunteer tend the plants.

13. If possible, gather or buy the various types of berries that the girls in the story found, (e.g., blackberries, raspberries, blueberries, and cranberries). Have children taste them for differences. How many uses can they think of for the berries? Perhaps the children might compile and distribute a "Berry Recipes Book."

14. Ma made Indian Pudding. Here is a recipe to try with the children:

4 cups milk	¼ teaspoon salt
1/3 cup corn meal	½ teaspoon ginger
¾ cup molasses	½ teaspoon cinnamon
¼ cup margarine	1 egg (beaten)
¼ cup sugar	maple syrup or whipped cream (optional)

Mix 4 cups of milk with the corn meal and cook for 15 minutes over a low flame, stirring constantly. Add the molasses and cook for 5 more minutes. Do not boil the mixture. Add the margarine, sugar, salt, and spices and mix until the margarine is melted. Slowly add the beaten egg to the mixture. Pour the mixture into a greased 2-quart baking dish. Bake at 350 degrees for 1½ to 2 hours, until firm. Serve with maple syrup or whipped cream, if desired.

15. Try this recipe for Quoddy Head fish chowder:

¼ pound of salt pork or bacon	4 cups milk
3 cups potatoes, diced	1 quart chicken stock
1 pound any fresh white fish	¼ cup margarine
(e.g., haddock, cod, orange roughy)	1 teaspoon salt
2 onions, diced	½ teaspoon pepper
2 stalks celery, diced	

Cut the salt pork or bacon into small pieces and fry. Drain the grease. Combine all the ingredients in a heavy kettle and simmer slowly for about 1½ hours, stirring occasionally. Do not boil the chowder.

16. Apples and cranberries would have been plentiful on Tibbetts Island. Use these fruits to make a New England Bundt Cake:

1¼ cups sugar	1 teaspoon cinnamon
1 egg	1 teaspoon nutmeg
1/3 cup cooking oil	½ cup coarsely chopped cranberries
1 cup flour	2 cups pared and diced apples
½ teaspoon salt	1 cup chopped walnuts (optional)
1 teaspoon baking soda	

Combine all the ingredients in a large bowl and blend thoroughly. Bake in Bundt or tube pan or in a well-greased 8-by-8-inch cake pan for 45 minutes at 350 degrees.

17. Have the children make a chart showing the four seasons. Have them list the chores that had to be done in the story during each season. Some chores may overlap two or even three seasons, and some jobs had to be done year round. Have children list the chores they do and compare the two lists.

18. Spruce boughs were laid against the foundation of the house as insulation against the cold weather. Discuss methods and materials that can be used as insulation today. Have each child bring to class materials that they believe will insulate an ice cube placed inside a zipper-locked plastic bag. Wrap the insulating material around the bag. After a specific amount of time has elapsed, unwrap the bag and measure the amount of water. The least amount of water indicates the best insulator. Have children rank the insulating materials from best to worst.

19. Have children compare the island at the beginning and the end of the story. Have them draw or narrate the changes that occurred from the time when Ma and Pa first came to the island until only Annie and little Matthias were left on the farm.

20. Have children pretend that they are one of the family members who has moved away from Tibbetts Island and has returned to the island after an absence of 30 years. Have them write a letter to another family member, describing the changes that have occurred on the island.

21. This story could have ended differently. Have children create a new scenario for the ending (e.g., What if Hannah had refused to move to the island? What if little Matthias's Pa had not died? What if the rusticators had not come to the island?). Have children role play their alternate endings.

22. A eulogy is a laudatory speech given at a funeral in honor of the person who had died. Have children write a eulogy in praise of Matthias. As a class, compare how the children remember this man.

23. In the library media center, have children read other books by Barbara Cooney, such as *Miss Rumphius* (see Chapter 11) and *Hattie and the Big Waves*. How did the marine environment affect the lives of the characters in these books? What were their childhoods like? How did they fulfill their drama?

24. Word Search— *Island Boy*
    Words from the story *Island Boy* are hidden in this word search—horizontally, vertically, and diagonally, forwards and backwards. First, match the words to the clues.

CLUES

a. The steadfast old man of Tibbetts Island

b. Summer visitors

c. The number of brothers

d. New growth on a baby bird's head

e. Insulation for the house

f. A gull-like sea bird

g. A large New England city

h. A feathery duck

i. It was used for sliding

j. Birds lay these

k. It was the color of the harbor

l. A sleeping spot for toddlers

m. The story takes place here

n. A gentle movement in the water

o. These were grown in the garden

p. It was cut to build fences and walls

q. A serious sickness

r. Matthias adopted this gull

s. A small boat

t. To chop down a tree

u. Matthias's daughter

v. A large black bird with webbed feet and a hooked bill

w. It was cut and harvested for refrigeration

x. A small grey-and-white shore bird

WORDS USED

Annie	eider	Matthias	swell
barrel stave	fell	pinfeathers	tern
Boston	flu	rusticators	Tibbetts Island
cormorant	green	six	Toad
dory	gull	spruce boughs	trundle bed
eggs	ice	stone	vegetables

From *Exploring the Environment Through Children's Literature.* © 1999 Butzow and Butzow. Teacher Ideas Press. (800) 237-6124.

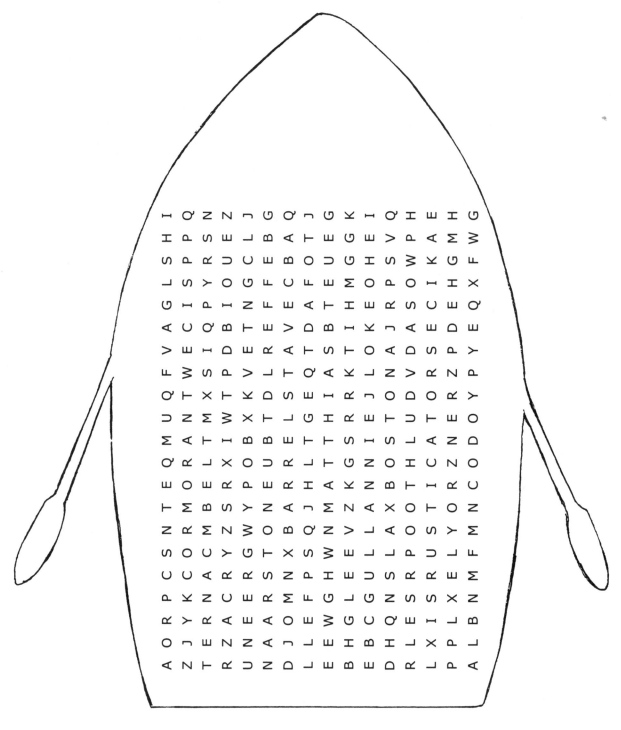

Fig. 10.5. Word Search—*Island Boy*.

From *Exploring the Environment Through Children's Literature.* © 1999 Butzow and Butzow. Teacher Ideas Press. (800) 237-6124.

Related Books and References

Cooney, Barbara. *Hattie and the Wild Waves.* New York: Viking Penguin, 1990.

———. *Miss Rumphius.* New York: Viking Penguin, 1982.

Fleagle, Gail. "Herbs Will Grow on You." *Science and Children* 31, no. 4 (January 1994): 12–15.

Kepler, Lynne. "Bloomin' Scientists." *Science and Children* 30, no. 4 (January 1993): 38.

Marturano, Arlene. "Horticulture and Human Culture." *Science and Children* 32, no. 5 (February 1995): 26–29+.

Rockwell, Anne. *The Way to Captain Yankee's.* New York: Macmillan, 1994.

Chapter 11

Environmental Awareness

Miss Rumphius

by Barbara Cooney
New York: Viking Penguin, 1982

Summary

Her goals were threefold—to visit faraway places, to live by the sea, and to beautify the earth. In her long life, Miss Rumphius was able to fulfill all her dreams. For many years she was a world traveler. Then she retired to her home by the sea where she spread lupine seeds far and wide.

Science and Content Related Concepts

Land use, environmental protection, environmental diversity, awareness of the environment, faraway places, beautification of the earth

Content Related Words

Figurehead, librarian, conservatory, travel, landforms, environment, mother-of-pearl, lupines

Activities

1. The pictures and the descriptions of the seashore indicate that this book probably took place in the state of Maine. Have children study these pictures of where Miss Rumphius lived, along with a road map of the state of Maine. How would they describe the geography of Maine? What occupations existed in Maine when Miss Rumphius lived there? Would these be the same today? What would the children expect Maine to look like if they could visit there today? To help with predictions, have children reread the book and search for answers in encyclopedias or tour guides of Maine.

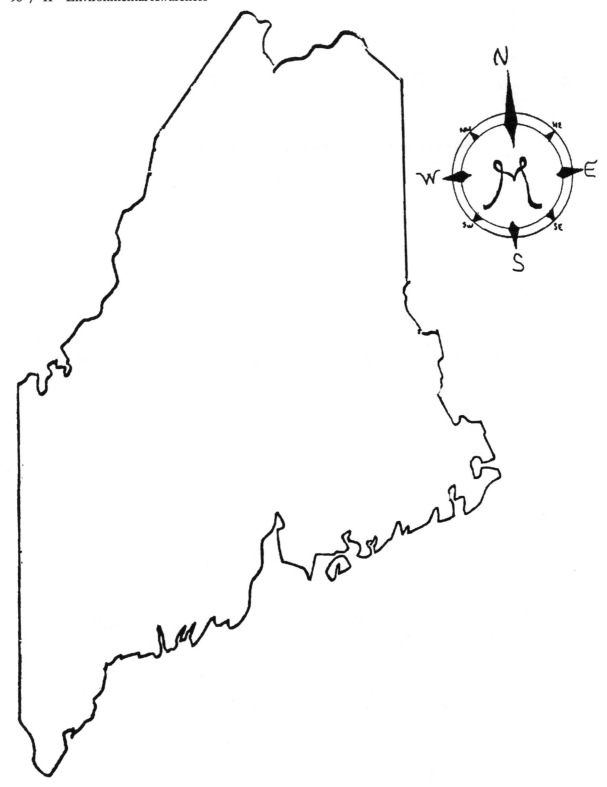

Fig. 11.1. Map of Maine.

From *Exploring the Environment Through Children's Literature.* © 1999 Butzow and Butzow. Teacher Ideas Press. (800) 237-6124.

2. In the library media center, have children locate pictures of sailing vessels that existed when Miss Rumphius was a young girl. The figurehead is the prominent wood carving on the prow of the boat—it usually resembles a person. Have the children design a figurehead of their own.

3. Miss Rumphius traveled to many environments (e.g., mountains, deserts, jungles, plains, tropical isles, rain forests, plateaus, wetlands). Divide the children into groups and assign a different environment to each group. The group will be responsible for researching the topic and providing information to other class members concerning landforms, climate, and vegetation of the area. If time permits, children should gather information about the people who live there and their culture. This information, along with a drawing or magazine photos of the environment, might be presented as a part of a classroom mural.

4. The book gives very general ideas of the environments where Miss Rumphius traveled. Have the children conduct research to generate a list of specific names and places to match the environments where she may have gone (e.g., the tropical isles could be the Fiji Islands of the South Pacific Ocean, or the mountains could be the Himalayas of northern India). Have children locate these places on a large map of the world. Are there any environments that Miss Rumphius did not see? NOTE: Vegetation, landform, and climatic maps may be of use for this activity.

5. Have the children pretend that they are Miss Rumphius. Have them select one of the environments she visited and describe it in a letter to her grandniece, who tells this story.

6. Plants are native to different environments around the world (e.g., ferns enjoy a warm, humid setting; cactus need a hot, dry, sandy place to grow). Invite someone who studies plants to speak to the class about various plants and the environments in which they best thrive. What type of soil is best for each plant? How much water is needed for best growth? What climate is necessary? What kind of fertilizer should be used? Is there a need for pruning or "pinching back" the plants? Because there are so many varieties of plants, the guest speaker may want to concentrate on indoor houseplants or plants that are typically found in flower beds near buildings (e.g., the lupine). NOTE: Some plants, such as the lupine, are cultivated in flower beds yet also grow wild.

7. Many people who enjoy gardening belong to gardening clubs. Are there any gardening clubs in the local area? If so, invite a member to speak to the class about gardening and some of the community projects that these clubs often adopt.

8. The lupine was a very special flower for Miss Rumphius. It is a perennial plant, which means that grows anew every year without being replanted. Have the children germinate and grow lupines in the classroom, then transplant them outdoors (see activity 9). As an experiment, vary the soil in which the seeds are planted (e.g., potting soil, claylike soil, sandy soil, vermiculite), but give the plants the same amounts of water and sunlight. Have the children keep plant journals showing the growth and development of their seeds. Do they think that the soil in which the seeds are planted accounts for the healthiness of the plant? Have children predict which plants will thrive and which will be unhealthy. NOTE: In this experiment, the amounts of water and sunlight given to the seedlings remain constant, but the kind of soil changes. The soil is the variable. Introduce children to the word *variable*. For an experiment to be effective, only one variable at a time should be manipulated.

Fig. 11.2. Lupines.

9. If the lupines that the children grow are strong and healthy, ask the principal if they can be transplanted outside the school. Before transplanting them, have the children map the school grounds and determine the best location for a flower garden. To prepare a flower bed for planting, it will probably be necessary to obtain assistance in digging from a school custodian or parent. Use the information learned in activity 6 when replanting the lupines and adding nutrients to the soil.

10. An ongoing project to accompany the previous activity is to have children plan an entire perennial garden, which would grow anew year after year. There are five steps to achieving a healthy garden:

    a. A perennial garden generally has three types of plants: tall flowers, such as lupines, which form the back of the garden patch; flowers of medium height, such as primroses, which are in the middle of the garden; and flowers of low height, such as English daisies, which form a border around the edge. NOTE: Depending on the time that the flowers bloom, children may not see the fruits of their work until they return to school in the fall. Be sure that all the children have a chance to see their flowers in September. Or, encourage children to visit the school grounds during the summer to see the flowers. Midsummer is usually the height of the flowering season, although lupines may bloom in early summer.

    b. One of the pleasures of growing flowers is seeing their many colors. When the children design their garden, have them decide whether the flower beds will consist of various colors of flowers or only one color. It is also possible to plan the garden based on when the flowers blossom, so that there will always be flowers in bloom. For example, children might select a flower that blooms in the early summer, such as the lupine; one that blooms in the later summer, such as the daisy; and so on.

    c. If there is adequate money available for the gardening project, it might be wise to buy some containers of different flowers that have already sprouted and are fully established. The plants should be about six to ten inches in height and should be planted so that the roots are deeply covered. Ask a nursery employee for additional information about planting the seedlings. NOTE: These seedlings are known as bedding plants, and are usually sold by the pack, the basket, or the flat.

The Perennial Garden

Fall Summer Spring

Fig. 11.3. Seasonal flower garden.

From *Exploring the Environment Through Children's Literature.* © 1999 Butzow and Butzow. Teacher Ideas Press. (800) 237-6124.

d. How much will it cost to plant a small perennial garden? Have children try this practice exercise: Assume that the garden will be rectangular in shape. The back row will consist of 12 lupines; in the middle row are 12 primroses; and in the front row are 12 English daisies. The prices of the seedlings are as follows:

Lupines cost 59¢ per plant, or $2.89 per six-pack.

Primroses cost 49¢ per plant, or $1.79 per four-pack.

English daisies cost 69¢ per plant, or $2.49 per four-pack.

What is the total cost of planting the garden? NOTE: If possible, find seed catalogs or ads for flower centers on the Internet so that you could compare prices.

e. The flower garden might be part of a larger project to beautify the school environment in many ways. Have children make suggestions by homeroom (e.g., obtaining new flags for the flagpole, refurbishing the playground equipment). Have a committee of teachers review these suggestions and choose which to implement. Select a coordinator to oversee the projects. A fund-raising project (e.g., selling pizzas, candy bars) or a grant from the school board may be necessary to complete these beautification projects.

11. When Miss Rumphius began scattering lupine seeds, people nicknamed her That Crazy Old Lady. Ask children why people called her this. Was this nickname positive or negative? How and when did she acquire the nickname Lupine Lady? What does this name suggest about the way people viewed her? Do children think that she liked this new name?

12. When she saw all the flowers that had grown along the seashore, Miss Rumphius thought that the birds were responsible for this. Ask children what is meant by the term *seed dispersal.* Why did Miss Rumphius believe that the birds had dispersed the seeds?

13. Miss Rumphius became a legend to the people who lived near her. In the library media center, have the children look up the word *legend.* Are they familiar with the legends of such figures as Johnny Appleseed and Paul Bunyan? Can a person who is alive be considered a legend during their lifetime? Who do children think will become a legend at some time in the future? Well-known sports figures and musicians are likely candidates.

14. Miss Rumphius had three dreams—to visit faraway places, to live by the sea, and to beautify the earth. Have children think of three dreams they have. The dreams may concern a future occupation, places the children want to go, or they may simply be appealing experiences. Have children make a drawing of these dreams to share with a friend. How will children attempt to realize their dreams? Use the dream pictures to make a bulletin board display.

15. Have children talk to older persons (e.g., parents, grandparents, great-aunts) about the dreams they had when they were young. Did they imagine visiting faraway places or living by the sea? Which dreams have come true? Which are they still hoping to realize? Have children share a dream of their own with these persons.

16. After many years as a librarian and a world traveler, Miss Rumphius "retired" to her seaside home. Have children discuss the plans she had for retirement. What actually happened? At what age do people retire in this society? What do they do when they no longer must work every day? Have children spend some time with a retired person and ask them about their life.

17. Have children compare the drawings in this book to those in *Ox-Cart Man* by Donald Hall (see Chapter 3) and *Island Boy* by Barbara Cooney (see Chapter 10). The illustrations in all three books were drawn by Barbara Cooney. How would children describe her style? What do they think of her use of color? Are the pictures realistic or impressionistic? In the library media center, have children look at other books by this author/illustrator and find the common characteristics present throughout.

18. Word Ladder—*Miss Rumphius*
    The answers to this word ladder are formed around the words *Miss Rumphius*. First, match the words to the clues.

CLUES

a. Lowlands along a waterway

b. Urban areas

c. High rises of land

d. Dense forests in the tropics

e. Places to grow crops

f. Low mounds of land

g. Extensive treeless expanses of land

h. Lands along the seacoast

i. Dense evergreen forests that receive a great amount of rain per year

j. Elevated, flat expanses of land

k. Dry, barren regions covered with sand

l. Landforms surrounded by water

WORDS USED

cities	mountains
deserts	plains
farms	plateaus
hills	rainforests
isles	river valleys
jungles	seashores

From *Exploring the Environment Through Children's Literature.* © 1999 Butzow and Butzow. Teacher Ideas Press. (800) 237-6124.

```
        M   __ __ __ __ __ __ __ __
        __ I __ __ __ __
     __ __ S __ __ __
  __ __ __ S __ __ __ __

__ __ __ __ __ __ R __ __ __
        __ U __ __ __ __ __
     __ __ __ M __
        P __ __ __ __ __
        H __ __ __ __
        __ I __ __ __ __ __ __ __ __ __ __
__ __ __ __ __ __ U __
        __ S __ __ __
```

Fig. 11.4. Word Ladder—*Miss Rumphius*.

Related Books and References

Cooney, Barbara. *Island Boy*. New York: Viking Kestrel, 1988.

Ehlert, Lois. *Planting a Rainbow*. San Diego, CA: Harcourt Brace Jovanovich, 1988.

Hall, Donald. *Ox-Cart Man*. New York: Viking Press, 1979.

Marturano, Arlene. "Horticulture and Human Culture." *Science and Children* 32, no. 5 (February 1995): 26–29+.

Roth, Susan. *Better Homes and Gardens Complete Guide to Gardens*. Des Moines, IA: Better Homes and Gardens Books, 1997.

From *Exploring the Environment Through Children's Literature*. © 1999 Butzow and Butzow. Teacher Ideas Press. (800) 237-6124.

Chapter 12

Forest Management

Mousekin's Lost Woodland

by Edna Miller
New York: Silver Burdett Press, 1996

Summary

Mousekin heard the crashing of trees all around him. Soon he was aware of the many changes in the forest: The beaver pond was gone, the animals no longer had places to feed, and there were strange figures building a house. However, the devastation of the forest caused by the building of this home was counteracted by the construction of a second house—one friendly to the environment.

Science and Content Related Concepts

"Wise use," conservation, woodland, ecological niche

Content Related Words

Conservation, ecology, beaver dam, chainsaw, habitat

Activities

NOTE: If possible, visit an area where the children can study plants and animals in their natural habitat. This study site should be about 20,000 square feet in size and should be an area not greatly altered by humans. Another possibility for a study site is to have a parent or other volunteer make a 10-minute videotape showing a natural area. Still another possibility is to obtain a commercial video of the outdoors from a nearby park or nature center. If a trip to visit a study site is not possible and a video cannot be obtained, the school grounds or a nearby park can be adapted to fit activities 1–4 of this unit. These activities assume that children are able to visit an outdoor site of some sort to work and learn.

1. Divide the class into five or six groups for the purpose of premapping the study site. Use string to mark each group's territory. Give each group a piece of paper and a clipboard, or a notebook. Each group should agree on the map symbols that they will use to map its plot of land. For example, a shaded round mark might be used to represent a tree; a checkmark might be used to represent grassland. After each group has finished studying the landforms and the plant and animal life of their plot of land, have the children draw a

sketch of their section of land on paper. The maps should show hills, rocks, water, and slope, as well as the plant and animal life. A video, which might be made during the mapping activity, can be of use in the classroom to review the overall area, as well as to zoom in on details. NOTE: Be sure that children follow appropriate safety rules and that there is one adult with each group. Children should not be allowed to wander away from their group, and the class should reassemble when all the groups have finished their mapping.

2. Back in the classroom, have children tape together their individual maps to form one large map (see fig. 12.1). Have children discuss the areas they saw and how they fit into the overall map. NOTE: If a video of the work done at the site is available, this is a good time to review it.

3. The third step of this activity is a simulation. Have children design a visitor center for the natural site that they have studied and mapped. Children should design a structure that can be built on the site with a minimal amount of disturbance to the natural features of the land, as well as to plants and animals. The visitor center is to serve as an orientation center for the study site, which is to be designated as a nature preserve. NOTE: If children are studying the school grounds or a nearby park, have them design a smaller structure (e.g., a travel-information kiosk, a small outdoor amphitheater for concerts, a picnic pavilion).

   a. Have the children continue working in their initial groups. Each group should design the entire interior of the building by drawing an aerial view of the structure. They should include an admission center, a gift shop, restrooms and a drinking fountain, a theater, three or four museum rooms, a luncheon area, and a parking lot. Children should indicate where the doors and windows will be placed, and where access for physically disabled persons will be built. The rooms should be drawn in relative size to one another (the theater will probably be the largest area; the admission center will probably be the smallest area). NOTE: Accompanying structures (e.g., shelters where sick or injured animals can be cared for until they are ready to return to the wild), if desired, should be planned as well.

   b. As a class, discuss the various layouts of the visitor center. What are the best features of the various sketches? What architectural and aesthetic pitfalls should be avoided?

   c. Once the interior of the visitor center has been designed and discussed, have each child draw a color picture of their impression of the exterior of the building. Remind children that the exterior of the building must reflect the plan for its interior, and that the building is to blend into the environment as much as possible. Landform features from the study site, such as trees and rocks, may be included in this drawing. NOTE: Written descriptions may be necessary to help explain the external design (e.g., Why is the exterior of the visitor center darkly colored?).

      The children might enjoy having an architectural competition to design the visitor center. Other teachers or the principal might be asked to be impartial judges for such a contest.

   d. To begin building a structure, various permits are usually required. Ask a local official to visit the class and discuss the construction of a local structure. Gather information about the following: zoning regulations, design approval, heat and electrical safety codes, water access and regulations, sewage and refuse disposal, approved building materials, accessibility regulations, and environmental effects. NOTE: Building codes and regulations differ from one area to another. Check the regulations governing the specific study site for this activity.

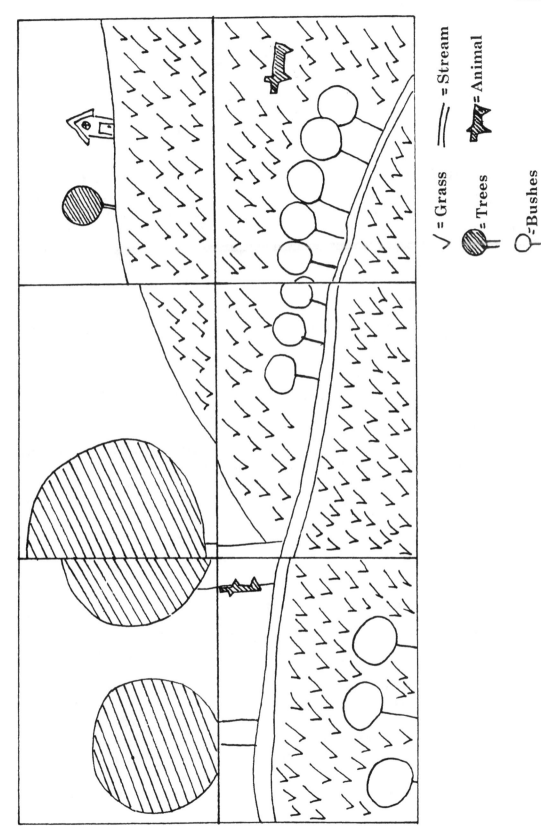

Fig. 12.1. Mapping an outdoor area.

√ = Grass
‖ = Stream
🐾 = Animal
● = Trees
○ = Bushes

From *Exploring the Environment Through Children's Literature.* © 1999 Butzow and Butzow. Teacher Ideas Press. (800) 237-6124.

4. Have children imagine that the new nature center they have designed is now open to the public. A person in charge of marketing has been chosen to advertise the center so that people will learn about it and come to visit. Have the children pretend to be this person and make a folder or brochure that will interest people in coming to visit the center. What will people be able to see there? Will there be activities to do? Are there forest animals at the center or nearby? Are videos, books, and souvenirs available? Is there an admission discount for tour groups? Children should add any other information that they think is important for visitors to know.

5. Listening to the sounds of the forest can be educational, as well as recreational. During a quiet time of the day, have the children listen to an audiocassette of woodland forest sounds. Can they recognize specific natural sounds or instruments? How do the sounds change to indicate different moods? Are some sounds relaxing? Do other sounds become more dramatic? What instruments are used to represent various moods or actions? Can they hear any elements of the weather? How might an audiocassette of rain forest sounds be different? Have the children compare the audiocassette of woodland forest sounds to one of city sounds. Which do they prefer?

6. City structures such a shopping malls often have a very devastating effect on the environment. For example, a large discount store for home builders decides to construct a local outlet. The first step in the development of the new complex is to cut down all the trees on the acquired property. Then the land is bulldozed flat and additional soil is brought in to be used as fill under the new parking lot. A nearby street may be expanded from two lanes to six lanes, and the lawns and gardens of many nearby homes must be built behind retaining walls to prevent erosion by rain. Are occurrences such as this happening locally? Are there any zoning rules that help protect the environment? Are there any local groups that lobby to help builders become more aware of the environment? Are there steps that might be taken after the buildings have been erected to improve the environment (e.g., planting a row of trees between a building and a nearby neighborhood)? What economic advantages might counteract some of the negatives feelings toward construction of a new structure? For example, would a new store engage in any service-oriented projects (e.g., the awarding of grant money for property beautification)? This activity could include discussion of the above points, possibly led by a local businessperson who could be for or against the project. If there is no such project, discuss the possibility of one. The teacher can also be the group leader.

7. Have children consult a detailed map of the state and locate the protected forest lands. More information about these lands can be obtained by telephoning the state agency in charge of these areas. These agencies, which are usually located in the state capital, may be called by various names (e.g., the Department of Forest Resources; the Department of Agriculture; the Department of Conservation; or, for national forests, the Department of the Interior, located in Washington, D.C.). Have children determine how much land is protected in their area. Before contacting the appropriate agency, have the children write down the questions that they want to have answered, including: What does *protected* really mean? Can people hunt and fish in these areas? What recreational areas exist within the boundaries of the forest? Are new areas being acquired to increase the amount of protected lands?

8. Trees are very useful to both humans and animals. Have each child describe what they think of when they hear the word *tree*. Categorize these responses into groups and construct a concept map (see fig. 12.2). Use lines to link ideas and relationships.

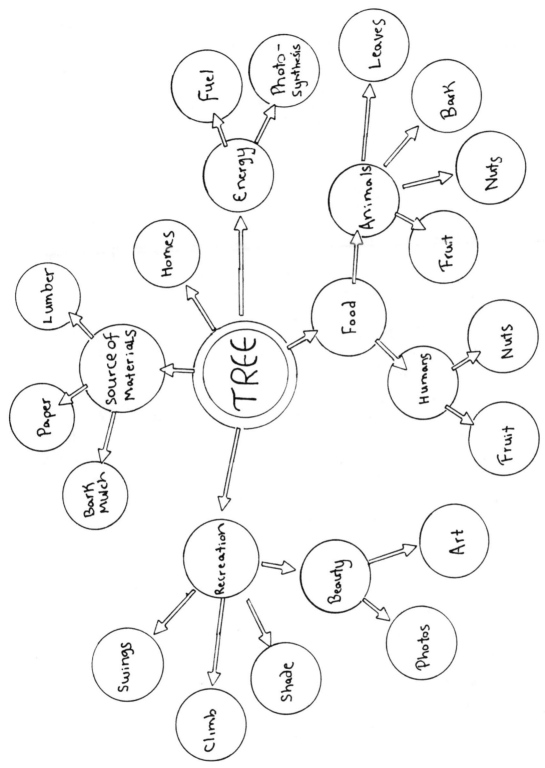

Fig. 12.2. Tree concept map.

From *Exploring the Environment Through Children's Literature.* © 1999 Butzow and Butzow. Teacher Ideas Press. (800) 237-6124.

9. In the story, Mousekin used items that he found on the forest floor to make a safe, comfortable nest. Have children draw a picture and write a description of their "nest"—the place where they can relax and be safe and happy.

10. Ask a library media specialist to help children find poems about nature, trees, animals, and so on. Have the children read these poems and then create their own poetry. It may follow a particular form, and can be either rhymed or unrhymed. For example, a child might brainstorm ideas about trees to make a list poem:

> A tree is a place to relax.
> A tree is a home to animals.
> A tree is wood and leaves.
> A tree is . . . .

11. The Department of Forest Resources operates as a branch of state government. Have students access the Website for the forest resources department from the state of Maine, then look for one from their state. Maine's Web site is http://www.state.me.us/doc/mfs/mfshome.htm.

12. Have students pretend that they are making up a list of books to be sold in the bookstore of the nature center. What books on nature would students find in the library media center to give them some ideas.

13. Word Scramble—Forest
    Unscramble the "forest" words below and match them to the clues.

soume	erde	rcacono	tabrib
eeb	xfo	kwah	hkpcimun
sifh	relriusq	low	laiqu
abveer	dopockrewe	fogr	daot
ruttel	osego	gollipow	

CLUES

a. It has a large bushy tail

b. It has stripes down its back

c. It builds dams in streams

d. It is known for its striped tail

e. It starts life as an egg deposited in wetlands

f. It can "drill" a hole into a tree's surface

g. It is a froglike land animal

h. It pollinates flowers in the forest

i. It is known for its manner of jumping

j. It is a long-necked water bird

k. It is a bird of prey

l. It is a nocturnal bird of prey with large eyes

From *Exploring the Environment Through Children's Literature.* © 1999 Butzow and Butzow. Teacher Ideas Press. (800) 237-6124.

m. It is a land-and-water reptile with a hard shell

n. It is hunted for its culinary qualities

o. It is a small, wild-doglike animal

p. It is a large, cud-chewing animal with antlers

q. It lives in water its entire life

r. It is a stage of the frog's life cycle

s. It is a small gnawing mammal

WORDS USED

beaver	fox	owl	squirrel
bee	frog	polliwog	toad
chipmunk	goose	quail	turtle
deer	hawk	rabbit	woodpecker
fish	mouse	raccoon	

Related Books and References

Tompkins, Peter, and Christopher Bird. *The Secret Life of Plants*. New York: HarperCollins, 1989.

Zim, Herbert, Alexander C. Martin, and Dorothea Barlowe. *Trees: A Guide to Familiar American Trees*. New York: Golden Books, 1987.

From *Exploring the Environment Through Children's Literature*. © 1999 Butzow and Butzow. Teacher Ideas Press. (800) 237-6124.

Chapter 13

Air Pollution

No Star Nights

by Anna Egan Smucker
New York: Alfred A. Knopf, 1989

Summary

There was a time when the pollution of the smokestacks from the steel factories obliterated the skyline of Pittsburgh and its surrounding towns. That way of life was not to last, though: The giant steel mills closed. Pittsburgh today is again a thriving center. New occupations have established dominion, and the Steel City is only a memory.

Science and Content Related Concepts

Iron- and steel-making processes, human environment, quality of life, change, industrialization, air pollution

Content Related Words

Pittsburgh metropolitan area, open-hearth furnace, molds, molten slag, thimbles, cranes, ingots, graphite, smog, thermos bottle

Activities

NOTE: Figure 13.1 will be used in the first three activities of this unit.

1. Have children locate the cities that were important to the author who wrote this book (e.g., Pittsburgh, Pennsylvania; Steubenville, Ohio; Weirton, Clarksburgh, and Bridgeport, West Virginia).

2. Central to the economic life of the Pittsburgh area was the availability of raw materials for the manufacture of iron—coal, limestone, and iron ore. Have children indicate on the map the states that were the sources of these raw materials:

    Coal—Pennsylvania, West Virginia, Ohio, Kentucky
    Limestone—Virginia, Pennsylvania, Ohio, Illinois, Michigan, Alabama
    Iron Ore—Minnesota, Wisconsin, Michigan, Alabama, New York, Pennsylvania

3. The most economical way of producing iron in the Pittsburgh area was to use iron ore from the Masabi Range in Minnesota. It was possible to transport this iron ore to Pittsburgh almost entirely through the use of waterways. Have children trace this series of waterways on the map. How might other raw materials have reached Pittsburgh?

4. Heavy pollution was a very real presence in the Pittsburgh area for many years. Is it possible to see pollution present in or around the school? One way to do this is to leave sheets of white paper lying around the classroom in places that will not be disturbed by children's everyday traffic patterns. After 10 to 14 days, have children carefully examine the papers using a hand lens or microscope. Have them count how many pieces of "pollution" lie in an area of one square inch on each sheet of paper. Which areas of the classroom are the dirtiest? Which areas are the cleanest? NOTE: See activity 13 in Chapter 4 for another way of gathering "pollution" that is particularly useful for outdoor situations.

5. Ask permission to have a class member wash the outside of one school window on each side of the building, using different cloths. What do the cleaning cloths look like after the washing? How do the cloths compare to each other? Why do the children suppose that this is so? Try this experiment again in three or four days, in the same place, and again after a week. What do the children conclude now? What is the source of the "pollution" that has been washed off the window?

6. Ask a library media specialist to help children find a book or encyclopedia articles about the iron-making industry. After studying the iron-making process (see fig. 13.2), have them place the following steps of the iron-making process in the correct order:

   a. Produce slag by removing impurities.

   b. Mine limestone.

   c. Mine iron ore.

   d. Burn the coke with iron ore and limestone.

   e. Mine coal.

   f. Retain the iron in the furnace and cast it into ingots.

   g. Heat and shape ingots in a forge or rolling mill.

   h. Heat the coal to make coke.

   NOTE: The first three steps are interchangeable; the others have a particular sequence.

7. Have the children create a skit or pantomime of actions that suggest the steps of the steel-making process.

8. Graphite is an important part of the iron industry. Children probably best know graphite as the "lead" in their pencils. In an encyclopedia, have them research the properties and the uses of graphite.

9. Have children work with their parents at home or with a library media specialist at school to make a list of products made of iron and steel (e.g., automobiles). Have children collect magazine photos of the objects or make their own drawings of these items. Make a classroom display or a bulletin board presentation for visitors or other classes to see. Discuss with children how life would be different without these items.

Fig. 13.1. Map of the eastern United States.

From *Exploring the Environment Through Children's Literature.* © 1999 Butzow and Butzow. Teacher Ideas Press. (800) 237-6124.

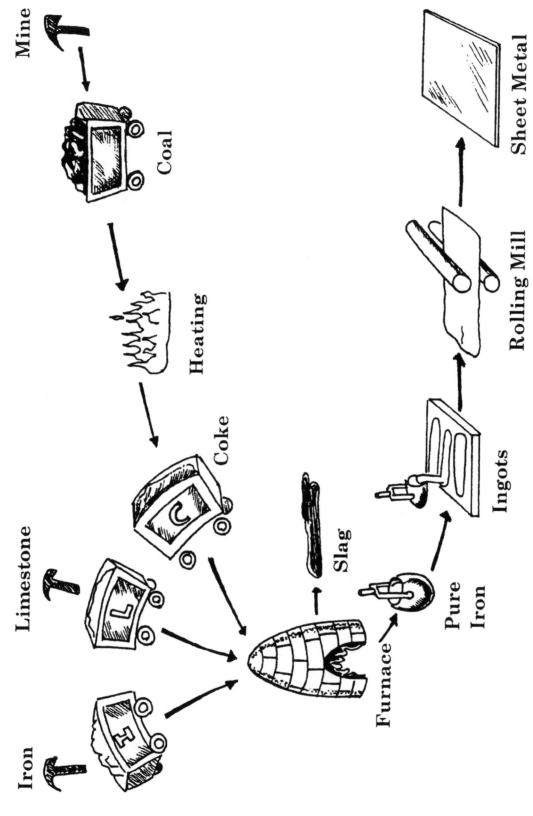

Fig. 13.2. The iron-making process.

From *Exploring the Environment Through Children's Literature.* © 1999 Butzow and Butzow. Teacher Ideas Press. (800) 237-6124.

10. Steel, a special form of iron, is formed into shapes by rolling, stamping, hammering, casting, or extruding it. Children can explore these same processes by working with dough. Dough can be hammered and rolled into crescents and other shapes, extruded into spaghetti with a pasta maker, stamped into shapes with cookie cutters, or "cast" into shapes with a mold. Have children simulate these activities in the classroom using the following simple dough:

    1½ cups water   2 teaspoons cooking oil
    ½ cup salt   2½ cups + 2 tablespoons flour
    2 teaspoons alum

    Mix the water with the salt. Place over heat and bring to boil. Remove from heat. Add alum and oil. Pour the hot mixture into a mixing bowl with flour. Mix and knead the dough for 5 minutes. Store the mixture in a plastic bag.

11. Steel is manufactured in many countries throughout the world. Which country produces the most steel? Which major country produces the least amount of steel? Using the information in the following list, have children rank the following steel-producing countries from the largest product to the smallest product. Have children make a bar graph to show this visually.

    The figures below are for world raw-steel production (the list is not exhaustive), given in millions of tons. The figures have been rounded off to the nearest million tons.

    United States (USA): 94 million tons   China (CHI): 93 million tons

    Canada (CAN): 14 million tons   Japan (JAP): 102 million tons

    European Union (EU): 155 million tons   India (IND): 20 million tons

    Latin America (LTA): 48 million tons   Confederation of Independent States (CIS) (countries of the former Soviet Union): 79 million tons

    Middle East (MDE) countries: 8 million tons

    Ask children where the United States is ranked on the graph. Who produces more steel than the United States? Was this always so? Have children research steel production for the United States and Japan about 20 years ago before the European Union. Where are France, Germany, and England on this list? What happened to steel production in the Soviet Union after the country divided into separate republics?

12. The pollution from the iron industry and the coal industry, once prevalent in the Pittsburgh area, was injurious to the lives of the residents living there. Most of the diseases that occurred as a result of the pollution were respiratory in nature. Ask a school nurse to speak to the class about respiratory diseases that are caused by pollution in the air.

13. Check a local telephone book for the toll-free listing for the American Lung Association in the area. Much information about respiratory diseases and smoking can be obtained at no cost. Additional information can be obtained from the national chapter of the American Lung Association at 1-212-315-8700. This group also tries to help students to understand the dangers of pollution and smoking, and can provide information about these topics. Have an adult contact this source for teaching materials on the dangers of pollution and smoking.

14. When the iron industry moved out of the greater Pittsburgh area, the metropolitan area surrounding the city also became economically depressed. Many of the workers were fired from their jobs, and there were no new jobs available for young workers. People could not make enough money to support their families and pay their bills. Ask children how their life would be different if they lived in an economically depressed area? Or, supposing they now live in an economically depressed area, how would their life be different if the economy improved? Discuss with children how these aspects of their life would change according to the economy: homes, stores, schools, churches, factories, transportation, and recreational facilities.

15. The Pittsburgh metropolitan area, which was once economically depressed, has since become a productive city. Ask children what they think is happening in cities such as Pittsburgh that improves the quality of life. What changes would they expect to see happening in Pittsburgh today (e.g., new office buildings, expanded airport facilities)?

16. Forbes Field, shown in *No Star Nights*, has been replaced by Three Rivers Stadium. Many other cities have seen a change in the stadium of their baseball team. Other teams move and expansion teams come into existence. As a means of reviewing American geography, have the children locate the cities of the American and National Baseball Leagues. Ask parents or children in other grades to help identify the names of the major-league teams and their locations. Write questions for children to answer based on the teams and their locations.

What is the direction from:

a. The Pittsburgh Pirates to the New York Yankees?

b. The Boston Red Sox to the Los Angeles Dodgers?

c. The Baltimore Orioles to the St. Louis Cardinals?

d. The Montreal Expos to the Florida Marlins (Miami)?

e. The Toronto Blue Jays to the Detroit Tigers?

f. The Philadelphia Phillies to the Seattle Mariners?

g. The Atlanta Braves to the Chicago Cubs?

What is the distance in miles between the following:

h. The New York Mets and the Tampa Bay Devil Rays?

i. The Milwaukee Brewers and the Minnesota Twins (Minneapolis)?

j. The Cincinnati Reds and the Colorado Rockies (Denver)?

k. The Kansas City Royals and the San Diego Padres?

l. The Oakland Athletics and the San Francisco Giants?

m. The Cleveland Indians and the Anaheim Angels?

n. The Houston Astros and the Chicago White Sox?

NOTE: Use the MapQuest program on the computer to make additional pairings. Estimate the distances before checking the answers. The pairing of two teams above does not necessarily mean that the two teams would be playing against each other. They are paired solely for the purpose of teaching geography. Expansion teams may be added to the exercise as they come into existence.

17. The trip to Forbes Field in the story was a major event in the lives of the children. Have the children choose an event that they attended and write a story about it. It might be a sporting event, a rock concert, a trip to an amusement park, or even a special television show when people gather together (e.g., the SuperBowl, a special showing of a movie.).

18. In the story, people spent their vacation money at "Christmas in July" sales. Ask a local retailer to speak to the class about when sales are held during the year. What kinds of sales are there (e.g., Presidents' Day sales)? How long do these sales last? How much can people probably save on sale days? How do people learn about such sales? During what sales period do merchants make the most of their money?

19. Parades are a large part of American culture. Have the children share this assignment with their parents: Write down the various local parades held each year. What is the purpose of each parade? When is it held? Who participates in the parade (e.g., youth groups, club members, bands, school groups, senior citizens)? Organize a small parade around the school in connection with a school holiday, a pet show, the principal's birthday, or any event that seems worthy of a parade.

20. Colors are important in this book. Have children experiment with these two challenges:

     a. The glow of the blast furnaces made the night sky appear in shades of red, orange, yellow, and rust. Make a portrait of the night sky.

     b. After the steel mills closed, the night sky appeared in shades of blue. Make a portrait of this night sky.

21. In the story, special days were celebrated with stuffed cabbage for dinner. Here is an old recipe to try:

Stuffed Cabbage (Holupki)

1 pound lean ground beef	Salt, pepper, and garlic powder, to taste
2 cups cooked rice	1 medium head cabbage
1 medium onion, finely chopped	1 cup beef stock, or 8 ounces tomato sauce

Mix the ground beef, rice, onion, and seasonings in a bowl. Submerge the head of cabbage in boiling water for about ½ hour. Drain the cabbage and let cool until it can be handled. Remove the core. Remove 12 leaves from the head of cabbage. Put about ¼ cup of the meat mixture onto a cabbage leaf and fold it up from the bottom, in at the sides, and over at the top of the leaf, envelope style. Place the rolls in a baking dish. Pour the beef stock or tomato sauce over the cabbage rolls. Cover with aluminum foil cook at 375 degrees for about 1½ hours, or until the cabbage is tender. Do not let the pan cook dry. NOTE: There will be leaves too small to peel off the head of cabbage. Shred these with a sharp knife and sauté them with cooked noodles and butter to make another ethnic dish from the Pittsburgh area, called haluski.

22. Word Search—*No Star Nights*

Words from the story *No Star Nights* are hidden in this word search—horizontally and vertically, forwards and backwards. First, match the words to the clues.

CLUES

a. The baseball team in the story

b. An enclosed chamber for melting iron ore

c. A building where steel was made

d. A strong metal used for making cars

e. Molten iron was poured from this container

f. Leftovers from the process of melting iron

g. Transportation used to go in and out of the mill

h. It signaled that it was time to stop working

i. The period of time that each man worked

j. It kept Dad's coffee hot

k. It could pick up heavy equipment

l. A bar of steel

m. Where the baseball team played

n. A tall container for helping smoke escape

o. The story took place near this city

p. Thimbles poured out a liquid called _____ _____

WORDS USED

crane	mill	shift	thermos
Forbes Field	molten iron	slag	thimble
furnace	Pirates	smokestack	train
ingot	Pittsburgh	steel	whistle

From *Exploring the Environment Through Children's Literature.* © 1999 Butzow and Butzow. Teacher Ideas Press. (800) 237-6124.

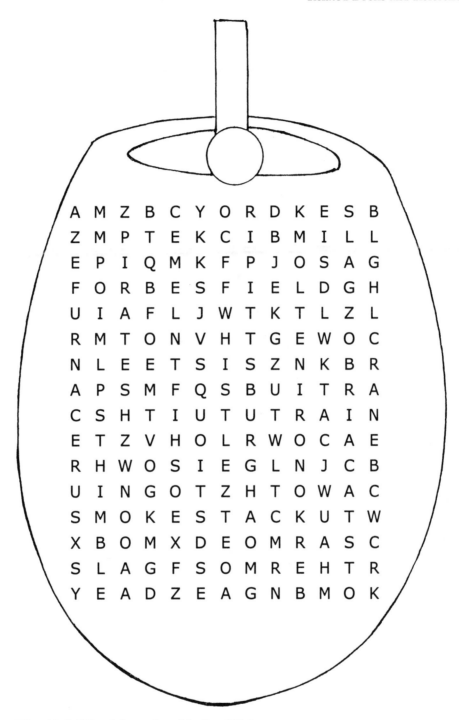

Fig. 13.3. Word Search—*No Star Nights.*

Related Books and References

Hendershot, Judith. *In Coal Country.* New York: Alfred A. Knopf, 1987.

From *Exploring the Environment Through Children's Literature.* © 1999 Butzow and Butzow. Teacher Ideas Press. (800) 237-6124.

Chapter 14

Solid Waste and Recycling

Just a Dream

by Chris Van Allsburg
Boston: Houghton Mifflin, 1990

Summary

After school, Walter tossed aside his donut wrappers and refused to sort the recycling items. That night, he dreamed of a world awash with litter and garbage. From then on, Walter was happy to do his part to maintain a clean, unpolluted environment and pledged to use resources wisely.

Science and Content Related Concepts

Conservation of resources, protection of the environment, decision making, recycling

Content Related Words

Ecology, ecosystem, stewardship, commitment, litter, pollution, biodegradable

Activities

1. To help save the environment, one must understand the problem of pollution and litter. Before beginning this unit, invite the children and their families to determine what role they play in this problem. Have each child tally the amount of trash that their family produces in one week for each of the categories listed below. List these items on a chart (see fig. 14.1). Include items that may be recycled because they are still part of the trash output of a family.

   a. Tin cans

   b. Plastic bottles

   c. Newsprint

   d. Plastic bags

   e. Paper bags

   f. Glass (brown, green, clear)

   g. Lawn clippings

   h. All other trash (number of bags)

123

Every "Litter" Bit Hurts

Tin Cans	Plastic Bottles	Newsprint	Plastic Bags
Paper Bags	Glass	Lawn Clippings	All Other Trash

Fig. 14.1. Pollution tally.

From *Exploring the Environment Through Children's Literature*. © 1999 Butzow and Butzow. Teacher Ideas Press. (800) 237-6124.

2. After a week of recording the amount of trash generated by each family, in the previous activity, tally the amount generated by the entire class. Discuss the amount of trash with the children and compare it to the estimated amount that the entire school or school district would generate. Of the amount of trash tallied, have children determine how much of it is recycled by government or private agencies. How much trash is left for disposal by nonrecycling methods?

3. After children have acknowledged the problem of trash disposal, contact the local government to determine what the community is doing to alleviate this problem. If possible, have someone from a local agency speak at a school assembly. Have the children prepare a list of questions that they want to have answered, including: Which items are collected by the community for recycling? Which items are picked up by private groups for recycling or disposal? Is there a recycling center to which items can be taken? Are the items collected for actual recycling, or are they disposed of in other ways? Is there a sanitary landfill for the nonrecycled trash? What about disposal of large items, such as dead tree branches or unusable appliances? Is there an educational program or literature available that explains what the community is doing to dispose of its trash? NOTE: This investigation into solid-waste disposal should include the part played by private as well as government organizations.

4. If the community has a recycling center, sanitary landfill, or waste disposal plant, arrange for the children to visit such a site. Have them prepare a list of questions to learn as much as possible during the visit. Investigate how school children can help keep the environment healthy.

5. Are there tasks that the class can do to help with the problem of solid-waste disposal at home, at school, or around the community? Have the children make posters to help explain their ideas to others in the school. Ask a local newspaper to print an article and photos to inform the community about the children's ideas.

6. A sanitary landfill is one way of disposing of all waste that cannot be recycled. Have children investigate how a landfill operates. Can it handle refuse such as plastic, household wastes, lawn clippings, medicinal waste, and industrial and atomic waste? Many states have little space left to build new landfills and would like to put them in adjoining states, where there may be more room or less stringent laws. Ask the children how they would feel if a more populated state wanted to build a landfill in their state. What would they think if a government agency wanted to bury atomic waste in their state? Debate the pros and cons of these situations.

7. Have children design a T-shirt (see fig. 14.2) or poster that illustrates their ideas about recycling and trash disposal.

8. Towns and cities are becoming more and more aware of the pollution problem that faces everyone. In some places, people are hired to manage solid-waste disposal. This person may hold a title such as Solid-Waste Enforcement Officer. This is a new job for most communities, so the job description for such an officer is often undeveloped. Have the children write a job description, pretending to be a member of a local council that needed to hire a person for this job. They should include a list of duties and responsibilities (e.g., to establish an educational program for grades K–3, to visit various landfills around the state to help plan a landfill in the district).

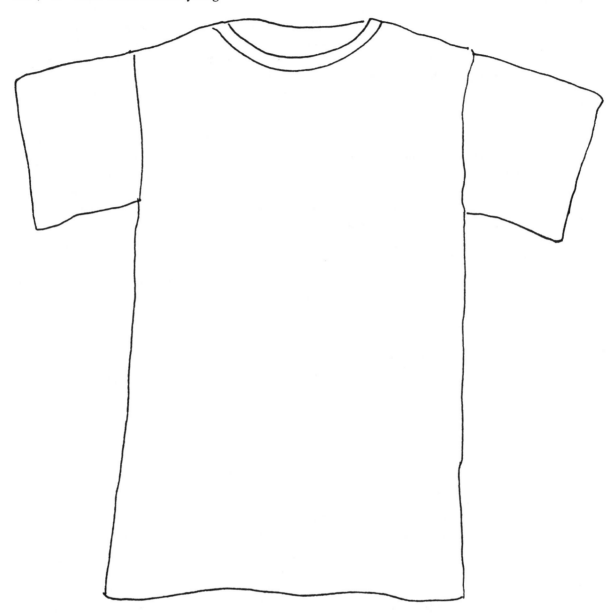

Fig. 14.2. T-shirt design.

From *Exploring the Environment Through Children's Literature.* © 1999 Butzow and Butzow. Teacher Ideas Press. (800) 237-6124.

9. In many states and cities, streets or highways are "adopted" by organizations, which then clean up the trash periodically. Contact the local government to determine whether it is possible for school children to adopt an area and keep it clean. This might be done by classes or by an after-school organization, such an "Earth Club" formed to learn more about the environment.

10. It is said that we are living in a "throw-away" society, in which items are used and then discarded. Items we use can be classified as single-use items or multiple-use items. Single-use items, such as paper plates and Styrofoam coffee cups, are also known as disposable items because they are used once and then thrown away. Multiple-use items, such as ceramic dinnerware and cloth hospital gowns, are cleaned and reused. A third category is often included—items that are used several times but are discarded when they break, such as wristwatches and computer boards, because it is less expensive to replace than to repair them. Have the class list items that are single-use, those that are multiple-use, and those that are discarded when broken. Should single-use items be replaced by multiple-use items? What are the advantages and disadvantages of each category of items? What are the economic incentives to reuse items or to halt the manufacture of goods that will become obsolete by the time they are sold?

11. In the book, Walter tosses away a donut wrapper as he walks home from school. Propose the following question to the children: Is it possible to map an area according to the trash found in the vicinity of various restaurants? Is there a path of discarded items that will reveal the foods the restaurants sell? Have the children look for litter such as soda cups, coffee cups, french-fry containers, paper wrappers, paper trays, and so on. How can the amount of trash that leaves a restaurant be reduced? How can restaurants encourage people to dispose of trash properly?

12. "A picture is worth a thousand words." The author of the story proves the truth of this saying by showing the future to Walter in a dream sequence. Have children select one of the pictures from Walter's dream and use it as the basis for writing a news article about the future. They should compose a headline for the piece to accompany their article. Children should also answer the questions Who? What? When? Where? and Why? to ensure that they have included the necessary details. The pictures from which children may select are the following:

The dump/landfill	The fishing fleet
The clear-cut forest	Highways
The factory smoke	Canyons
Mt. Everest Hotel	

13. A realistic look at Walter's future included such practices as hanging laundry to dry and using a hand-powered lawnmower. In classroom groups, have the children brainstorm other means by which people might contribute to a cleaner, healthier environment in the future. They should think of ideas that are environmentally sound and sensitive (i.e., things that will not pollute the air and the water or contribute to the amount of trash produced). Things that might be changed to produce a cleaner future environment include cars, homes, power generation plants, and clothing. Have the groups draw pictures of what they think the future will hold for society and then share their ideas with one another.

After children have brainstormed future ways to ensure a cleaner environment, in the previous activity, have them formulate their ideas into a written paper about what they think life will be like in the future for Walter, as well as for themselves.

14. Have children read an interview with Chris Van Allsburg at this Web site: http://www.eduplace.com/rdg/author/index.html.

15. Ask the library media specialist to help children find information on sanitary landfills—how they are made, who maintains them, do they smell, etc.?

16. Renewable resources are those which are continually replenished and do not run out. Nonrenewable resources are those which are used up and cannot be replaced. Discuss with children whether items in the list below are renewable or nonrenewable.

air	electricity (coal-generated)	natural gas	trees
coal	electricity (water-generated)	ocean tides	water
copper	fish	paper	wheat
cotton	gasoline	petroleum	wind
cows	glass	plastic	wool
diamonds	iron ore	soil	

17. Crossword—*Just a Dream*

CLUES

Across

1. "Every litter bit _____"
3. If it is _____, it will decompose in the environment
6. To rot
8. To use foolishly; trash or garbage
11. The act of saving; not wasting
13. Paper and trash scattered along streets and roads
14. The study of relationships between organisms and the environment
15. Impurities in environment

Down

1. The place where an organism lives
2. They often pollute the air
4. The act of rotting or decaying
5. Species in danger of becoming extinct are called _____
7. All that surrounds someone or something
9. An ecological community
10. Trash; often found in outer space, as well
12. To reuse

WORDS USED

biodegradable	ecology	factories	litter
conservation	ecosystem	habitat	pollution
decay	endangered	hurts	recycle
decomposition	environment	junk	waste

From *Exploring the Environment Through Children's Literature.* © 1999 Butzow and Butzow. Teacher Ideas Press. (800) 237-6124.

Fig. 14.3. Crossword—*Just a Dream*.

From *Exploring the Environment Through Children's Literature.* © 1999 Butzow and Butzow. Teacher Ideas Press. (800) 237-6124.

Related Books and References

Brittain, Alexander N. "Garbage Grows Great Plants." *Science and Children* 33, no. 7 (April 1996): 20–22.

DeFina, Anthony. "Environmental Awareness." *The Science Teacher* 62, no. 6 (September 1995): 33–35.

Faivre, Gerri. "Start Shredding the News." *Science and Children* 30, no. 4 (January 1993): 13–15.

Kepler, Lynne. "How Much Paper?" *Science and Children* 29, no. 5 (February 1992): 44.

———. "Know Your Plastics." *Science and Children* 30, no. 3 (November/December 1992): 62.

Sumrall, William J., and Gene Aronin. "Environmental Empowerment. "*The Science Teacher* 60, no. 2 (February 1993): 38–41.

Swarthout, Flora L. "The Science of Composting." *The Science Teacher* 60, no. 6 (September 1993): 27–29.

Vandas, Steve. "How Do We Treat Our Wastewater?" *Science and Children* 29, no. 8 (May 1992): 18–19.

Chapter 15

Effects of Environmental Change

The Wump World

by Bill Peet
Boston: Houghton Mifflin, 1970

Summary

The Wumps were happy creatures who thrived on grass and bumbershoot trees. When the Pollutians arrived from their worn-out planet, the Wumps hid underground, where they lived on mosses and mushrooms. After the Pollutians had overused and polluted the Wump World, they fled to another, cleaner planet. The Wumps were able to come out of hiding, but life would never be the same for them.

Science and Content Related Concepts

Industrialization, pollution, depletion of resources, environmentalism

Content Related Words

Pollution, habitat, environment, factory, industry

Activities

1. The Wumps did not resist the coming of the Pollutians. Instead, they adapted to their plight by finding a new home underground. Have children create a skit to show the actions of the Wumps and the Pollutians. How did each group make use of the environment?

2. In small groups, have children discuss what the Pollutians did to the Wump World. Assign one group the task of discussing what the Pollutians did to the "air" of the Wump World. Another group should discuss how "space" was affected. Other groups should discuss what the Pollutians did to the land, the water, the energy, and the vegetation. Use this information to construct a table that compares the two groups.

	Pollutians	Wumps
Air		
Space		
Land		
Water		
Energy		
Vegetation		

3. One of the problems that plagued the Pollutians resulted from their building a city without any regard to the future. They "used up" resources that could not be renewed. Once the space was gone, there was no way to find new space except by destroying their city. Once the water was polluted, years of cleanup would have been required to use the water again. Have children discuss how people on this planet guard against "using up" air, space, water, land, energy, and vegetation.

4. What are the differences between renewable and nonrenewable resources? Have children draw pictures of resources being renewed (e.g. planting trees to replace those that have been cut down, using garbage to make a fuel that can power vehicles).

5. It is instructive for children to compare the actions of the Wumps and the Pollutians. Below is a list of adjectives that apply to the characters in the book. Which adjectives describe the Wumps? Which describe the Pollutians? Have the children think of other words to describe the two groups. Discuss any differences of opinion in making the two lists. NOTE: This activity is a good opportunity to introduce the use of a thesaurus.

adventuresome	nonheroic
aggressive	overjoyed
frenzied	passive
frightened	peaceful
greedy	timid

6. The Pollutians showed concern only for the building of skyscrapers and transportation systems. They did not value natural beauty and did not plan for anything such as parks or recreational areas. Have children use an area map of the community or take a walk near the school to determine how the land is used. Do they find residential areas, industrial zones, business sectors, and farming areas? What areas have been reserved for schools, parks, recreational facilities, and museums?

From *Exploring the Environment Through Children's Literature.* © 1999 Butzow and Butzow. Teacher Ideas Press. (800) 237-6124.

7. There are probably various different zones of development in the community. If possible, have children visit sites in some of these zones (e.g., an industry, a farm, an office building, a convenience store). Have them draw pictures of what they saw and assemble them to form a paper quilt of the community.

8. Ask children if a sense of beauty is evident in the community. Are buildings pleasing to the eye and not just utilitarian? Is the community free from pollution and trash? Are the farms free of any clutter? Are there areas such as parks, gardens, and sports arenas that add beauty to the area? Is there evidence of community planning (e.g., no fast-food restaurants in the middle of a residential area, no industries in the middle of a downtown shopping district)?

9. In many towns and cities, there is much evidence of urban cleanup, rebuilding, and renovation. This is known as urban development or urban renewal. Ask a speaker who represents the local government or business community to talk to the class about how the community is renewing itself or what plans are being made for such a venture. What precautions are being taken so that the community does not become like the world of the Pollutians? How are resources used wisely? Who is making the decisions that guide this development and regrowth? What sources of funding are being used accomplish this task?

10. One of the most important things to think about as children try to understand the events of the book is its ending. Life might have been extremely different for the Wumps and the Pollutians if there had been a different ending to the story. Have children brainstorm some other ways that the book might have ended. Do they agree with the possibilities listed below?

    a. The Pollutians continue their destruction of the environment, including the underground habitat of the Wumps.

    b. The Pollutians see the folly of their ways and clean up the environment.

    c. The Wumps organize themselves and convince the Pollutians that the environment must be saved.

    d. Through hard work, the Wumps reclaim their world with the help of others. For example, the Wump World is colonized by loving, caring creatures who appreciate the Wumps' way of life and help clean up and save the environment. If children introduce new creatures into the story, have them name these creatures and draw pictures of them. Children should describe the lifestyle of these creatures (e.g., the food they eat, the clothing they wear, their forms of recreation) to better understand their role in the story.

11. The Pollutians were opportunistic in their use of the Wump World. They built and polluted with no intention of staying in their new city. They used the land and then left. Ask children what would have happened had there not been new worlds to inhabit. Would the Pollutians have changed their attitudes and behaviors so that they could stay in the Wump World forever?

12. Science fiction stories often concern a city that exists underground or on another planet. Have children invent a city that could exist in one of these settings. What would they need to provide (e.g., an air supply for breathing) so that creatures could survive there? What rules would be needed to manage the use of air, space, land, water, energy, and vegetation? How would the creatures that inhabit this city protect against pollution and

overuse of resources? Have children draw a sketch of their futuristic city, including buildings, streets, transportation systems, shops, hotels, recreational areas, and so on, and then make a collage of scenes from the city. How does it differ from the city of the Pollutians?

13. Some newspapers and television stations report a daily pollution index. Have children monitor this index for several days. Is there a visual difference in the air when the index is higher or lower? Do allergy sufferers notice a difference as the index changes? Does pollution affect exposure to the sun? How do changes in the index relate to changes in the weather (e.g., a higher pollution index results when the weather is overcast)? What are the sources of the pollution? Can it be decreased?

14. Refer to the units on *Just a Dream* (Chapter 14), *The Little House* (Chapter 4), and *A River Ran Wild* (Chapter 8). They contain many activities about pollution that can be used in connection with *The Wump World*.

15. Ask the library media specialist to set up a display of books about pollution for the class to use. These could be both fictional and nonfictional works.

16. Using a word processor, create a list of do's and don'ts to help children care for the environment.

17. Word Matching—*The Wump World*
    Review the characters and the actions that are part of *The Wump World*. Identify the creatures, places, and things described below.

    a. I am a tiny planet, smaller than Earth, with no oceans, mountains, or broad deserts.

    _____

    b. We are simple grass-eaters who spend most of our time grazing on the tall, slender grass.

    _____

    c. I am an old worn-out planet from which the Pollutians left.

    _____

    d. We are beings who develop lands without concern for the future.

    _____

    e. I am the leader of the Pollutians.

    _____

    f. I am the national symbol of the Pollutians. I appear on their flag.

    _____

    g. We are what the Wumps ate underground.

    _____

h. We are special trees that the Wumps love to nibble.

_____

i. We are what the Pollutians put into the streams and rivers.

_____

j. We are what the Pollutians put into the air.

_____

k. We are the three beings who coordinated the Pollutians' travel.

_____

l. I am where the Pollutians came after they left the Wump World.

_____

a bigger and better world	the Wumps
Wump World	waste, trash, pollution
the Outer Spacemen	the World Chief
smoke, fumes, pollution	mushrooms and green moss
three smokestacks	the Pollutians
Pollutus	bumbershoot trees

Related Books and References

Burton, Virginia Lee. *The Little House.* Boston: Houghton Mifflin, 1942.

Cherry, Lynne. *A River Ran Wild.* San Diego, CA: Harcourt Brace Jovanovich, 1992.

Kawecki, Nancy Nega. "Analyzing Air Quality." *Science Scope* 20, no. 5 (February 1997): 20–23.

Maguire, Brian. "Introducing I.M. Mr. Treeless." *Science and Children* 29, no. 7 (April 1992): 21–22.

Sparks, David. "Mission: New Earth." *Science Scope* 20, no. 5 (February 1997): 13–15.

Van Allsburg, Chris. *Just a Dream.* Boston: Houghton Mifflin, 1990.

Wolf, JoAnne. "Count Down to Earth Day." *Science and Children* 29, no. 7 (April 1992): 23–24.

From *Exploring the Environment Through Children's Literature.* © 1999 Butzow and Butzow. Teacher Ideas Press. (800) 237-6124.

Appendix

Answer Keys

Chapter 1—*The Land of Gray Wolf*

ACTIVITY 12 ANSWERS

Producers	Consumers	Decomposers
algae	birds	bacteria
bushes	bugs	fungi
grass	chipmunks	
plants	foxes	
trees	frogs	
	grubs	
	humans	
	rabbits	
	snakes	
	squirrels	
	worms	

ACTIVITY 20 ANSWERS

a. To create more foraging space for the deer, Gray Wolf and the men burned the _____.   land

b. When the European settlers came, they offered to _____ with the Indians.   trade

c. The European settlers really wanted to _____ the Indians from the land.   remove

d. Soon after the European settlers arrived, they _____ down the forest and converted the land to _____.   cut, farmland

e. When the Indians hunted, they killed only the number of animals necessary for _____ and _____.   food, clothing

f. The European settlers and the Indians were in conflict because the Indians used the land primarily for _____, while the European settlers used it for _____.   hunting, farming

g. The two cultures had entirely different ideas about land use. The Indians said that the land was for _____, while the European settlers said that it could be owned by _____.   everyone, individuals

h. The European settlers marked off plots of land using _____.   stone walls

i. When the land no longer produced good crops, the European settlers _____ and the farmland again became _____.   moved away, forest

Words with similar meanings are acceptable (e.g., *woods* for *forest*, *left* for *moved away*).

Chapter 2—*Brother Eagle, Sister Sky: A Message from Chief Seattle*

ACTIVITY 22 ANSWER

The answer to the math puzzle is "We belong to Earth."

Chapter 3—*Ox-Cart Man*

ACTIVITY 18 ANSWERS

Actions	Objects
1. weave	a. linen
2. spin	j. yarn
3. knit	b. mittens
4. harvest	m. fruit
5. gather	c. feathers
6. sheer	k. sheep
7. pick	l. turnips
8. dip	h. candles
9. split	g. shingles
10. carve	d. brooms
11. boil	f. sap
12. dig	i. potatoes
13. saw	e. planks

ACTIVITY 19 ANSWERS

Across

4. To cut wool from sheep   shear
6. These farmers follow the old ways   Amish
7. The market was in this town   Portsmouth
9. These handmade items gave off light   candles
11. A wooden vehicle for carrying goods   cart
12. It enabled the ox to pull a cart   yoke

14. Liquid tapped from the maple tree   sap
15. A sweet substance produced by bees   honey

Down

1. Used to sweep the floors   broom
2. They were stuffed into pillows and quilts   feathers
3. To turn yarn into mittens   knit
5. Roof coverings   shingles
7. Pieces of wood used for building homes and barns   planks
8. The source of wool fiber   sheep
10. A wheel was used to _____ fiber into yarn   spin
13. The story probably takes place here (abbr.)   NH

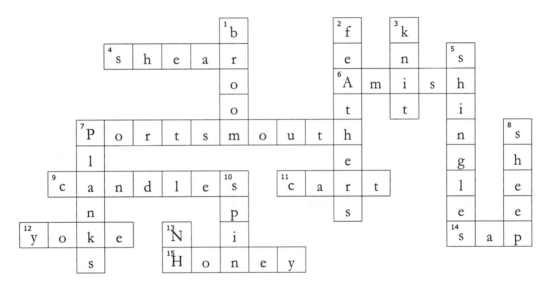

Fig. 16.1. Crossword—*Ox-Cart Man*.

Chapter 4—*The Little House*

ACTIVITY 15 ANSWERS

1.   d.   The Little House lives in the country.
2.   f.   City lights shine in the distance.
3.   a.   A horse and buggy drive by.
4.   j.   A paved road is built.
5.   c.   Gas stations and small houses are built.
6.   i.   Apartment houses and street lamps appear.
7.   g.   Trolley cars pass in front of the Little House.
8.   e.   Elevated trains travel back and forth.

9.   h.   Skyscrapers surround the Little House.

10.   b.   The Little House is moved to the country.

ACTIVITY 21 ANSWER

The Little House Maze

Fig. 16.2. Solving the maze.

Chapter 5—_Earthdance_

ACTIVITY 19 ANSWER

The answer to the math puzzle is "For you are home; you are precious Earth."

Chapter 6—_Water Dance_

ACTIVITY 7 ANSWER

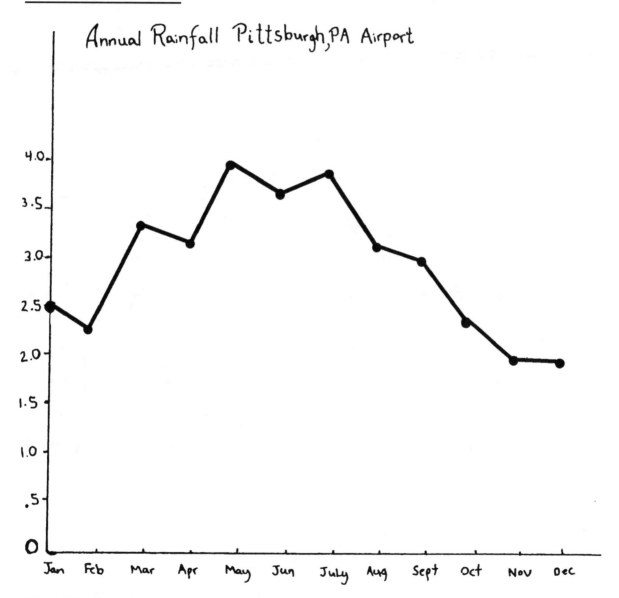

Fig. 16.3. Monthly precipitation graph.

ACTIVITY 17 ANSWERS

a. Vaporlike water   mist

b. Cascading waters   waterfall

c. An ocean   sea

d. A landlocked body of water   lake

e. Falling droplets of water   rain

f. A small amount of flowing water   stream

g. Storm cloud producing thunder   thunderhead

h. A mass of vapor in the sky; patterns of moisture   clouds

i. Colors formed by sunlight reflecting off rain   rainbow

j. Strong wind, with rain or snow   storm

k. A large stream   river

l. An abrupt change in air pressure, usually accompanied by wind and rain   storm front

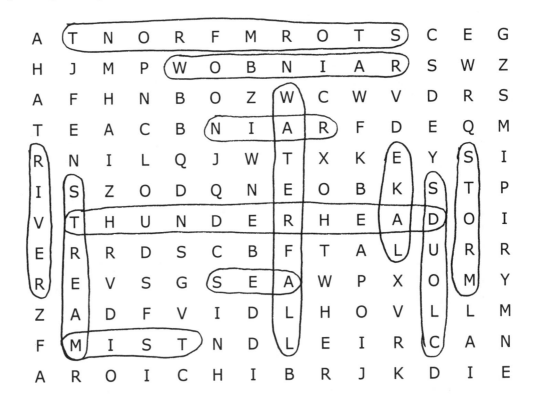

Fig. 16.4. Word Search—*Water Dance*

Chapter 7—*Letting Swift River Go*

ACTIVITY 19 ANSWER

The answer to the math puzzle is "You have to let them go."

Chapter 8—*A River Ran Wild*

ACTIVITY 14 ANSWERS

a.	A mountain near the Nash-a-way	Mt. Wachusett
b.	Dirty air and water	pollution
c.	A lady who spoke against polluting the river	Marian
d.	An Indian crop	corn
e.	Today's name for the river in the story	Nashua
f.	An animal that builds dams in the river	beaver
g.	Fish that live in clean waters	salmon
h.	A place for exchanging goods	trading post
i.	Settlers brought these to trade with the Indians	mirrors
j.	The Nash-a-way was known as the river with the _____ _____	Pebbled Bottom
k.	Machines were first used during the _____ Revolution	Industrial
l.	This animal is related to the deer	moose
m.	An object that helps one do work more easily	machine
n.	The leader of the Indians in the story	Chief Weeawa
o.	They were used for thatching roofs on homes	cattails
p.	To go, uninvited, on someone else's property	trespass

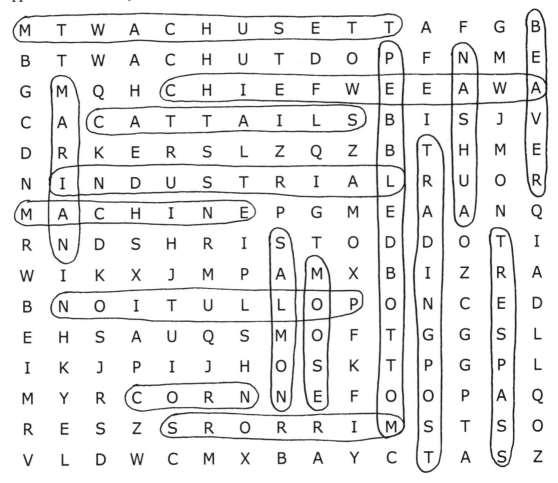

Fig. 16.5. Word Search—*A River Ran Wild.*

Chapter 9—*Flood*

ACTIVITY 27 ANSWERS

a.	To go over the banks of a river	overflow
b.	The greatest height to which the water rises	high water mark
c.	He or she warns people to leave their homes in an emergency	sheriff
d.	The direction from which the water flows	upstream
e.	The longest river in the United States	Mississippi
f.	A tributary leading to the Mississippi	Missouri
g.	To leave home and seek shelter	evacuate
h.	They are piled up to increase the height of the levee	sandbags
i.	He or she reports the weather news	forecaster
j.	Sarajean's family fled to safety in this	johnboat

k. An earthen wall built to prevent floods   levee

l. The point at which flooding begins   floodstage

```
A   C  (T   A   O   B   N   H   O   J)  D   F   H
M  (M   D   Q   R  (O   V   E   R   F   L   O   W)
F   I   C   A   R   M   A   R   I   N   O   P   Q
J   S  (E   G   A   T   S   D   O   O   L  (F)  Z
A   S   D   F   A   G   B   Z   H   F   I   O   J
(H   I   G   H   W   A   T   E   R   M   A   R   K)
U   S   V   W  (E   V   A   C   U   A   T   E)  J
K  (S   A   N   D   B   A   G   S)  R   N   C   Q
(M   I   S   S   O   U   R   I)  Q   S   L   A   H
M   P   O   T   P  (F   F   I   R   E   H   S)  N
(U   P   S   T   R   E   A   M)  V   A   F   T   O
G   I   H   J   L   N   P   E   Q   S   P   E   U
A   F   M   B   N   P  (E   C   O   E   D   R)  T
```

Fig. 16.6. Word Search—*Flood*.

Chapter 10—*Island Boy*

ACTIVITY 8 ANSWERS

a. Grays Head

b. Goat Island

c. Starbuck

d. Heart Island

e. Ocean Point

f. Sharp Point

NOTE: The directions below are only one possibility; other correct answers exist.

g. Sail 1¾ miles southeast, then 3 miles north.

h. Sail 3 miles east and 1 mile south.

i. Sail 3 miles south and 3 miles southwest.

j. Sail 2¼ miles south then 1 7/8 miles west.

k. Sail 4 miles south then 3½ miles west.

l. Sail 2¼ miles east, then 1¼ miles north.

ACTIVITY 24 ANSWERS

a.	The steadfast old man of Tibbetts Island	Matthias
b.	Summer visitors	rusticators
c.	The number of brothers	six
d.	New growth on a baby bird's head	pinfeathers
e.	Insulation for the house	spruce boughs
f.	A gull-like sea bird	tern
g.	A large New England city	Boston
h.	A feathery duck	eider
i.	It was used for sliding	barrel stave
j.	Birds lay these	eggs
k.	It was the color of the harbor	green
l.	A sleeping spot for toddlers	trundle bed
m.	The story takes place here	Tibbetts Island
n.	A gentle movement in the water	swell
o.	These were grown in the garden	vegetables
p.	It was cut to build fences and walls	stone
q.	A serious sickness	flu
r.	Matthias adopted this gull	Toad
s.	A small boat	dory
t.	To chop down a tree	fell
u.	Matthias's daughter	Annie
v.	A large black bird with webbed feet and a hooked bill	cormorant
w.	It was cut and harvested for refrigeration	ice
x.	A small grey-and-white shore bird	gull

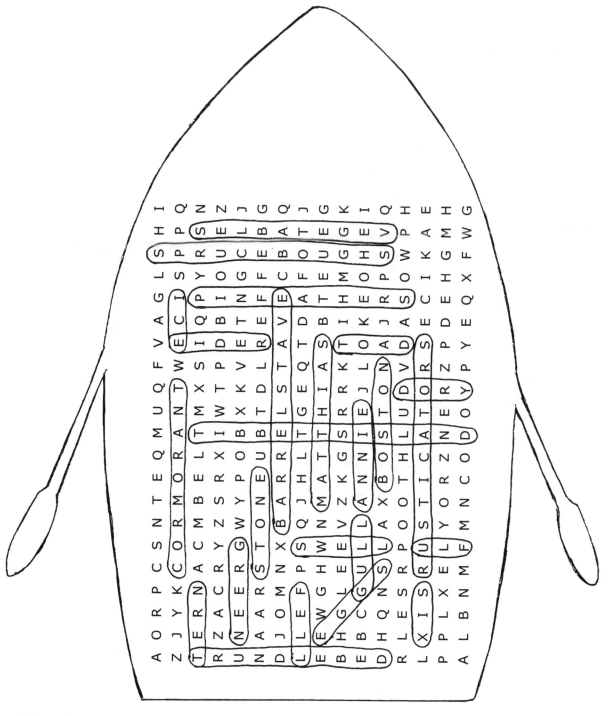

Fig. 16.7. Word Search—*Island Boy*.

Chapter 11—*Miss Rumphius*

ACTIVITY 10 ANSWER

The cost of a perennial garden is $18.62

ACTIVITY 18 ANSWERS

a.	Lowlands along a waterway	river valleys
b.	Urban areas	cities
c.	High rises of land	mountains
d.	Dense forests in the tropics	jungles
e.	Places to grow crops	farms
f.	Low mounds of land	hills
g.	Extensive treeless expanses of land	plains
h.	Lands along the seacoast	seashores
i.	Dense evergreen forests that receive a great amount of rain per year	rainforests
j.	Elevated, flat expanses of land	plateaus
k.	Dry, barren regions covered with sand	deserts
l.	Landforms surrounded by water	isles

M OUNTAINS

C *I* TIES

DE *S* ERTS

SEA *S* HORES

RAIN FO *R* ESTS

J *U* NGLES

FAR *M* S

P LAINS

H ILLS

R *I* VER VALLEYS

PLATEA *U* S

I *S* LES

Chapter 12—*Mousekin's Lost Woodland*

ACTIVITY 13 ANSWERS

a.	It has a large bushy tail	squirrel
b.	It has stripes down its back	chipmunk
c.	It builds dams in streams	beaver
d.	It is known for its striped tail	raccoon
e.	It starts life as an egg deposited in wetlands	frog
f.	It can "drill" a hole into a tree's surface	woodpecker
g.	It is a froglike land animal	toad
h.	It pollinates flowers in the forest	bee
i.	It is known for its manner of jumping	rabbit
j.	It is a long-necked water bird	goose
k.	It is a bird of prey	hawk
l.	It is a nocturnal bird of prey with large eyes	owl
m.	It is a land-and-water reptile with a hard shell	turtle
n.	It is hunted for its culinary qualities	quail
o.	It is a small, wild-doglike animal	fox
p.	It is a large, cud-chewing animal with antlers	deer
q.	It lives in water its entire life	fish
r.	It is a stage of the frog's life cycle	polliwog
s.	It is a small gnawing mammal	mouse

Chapter 13—*No Star Nights*

ACTIVITY 6 ANSWERS

Step 1–3: Choices b., c., and e. can appear in any order.
Step 4: h.
Step 5: d.
Step 6: a.
Step 7: f.
Step 8: g.

ACTIVITY 11 ANSWER

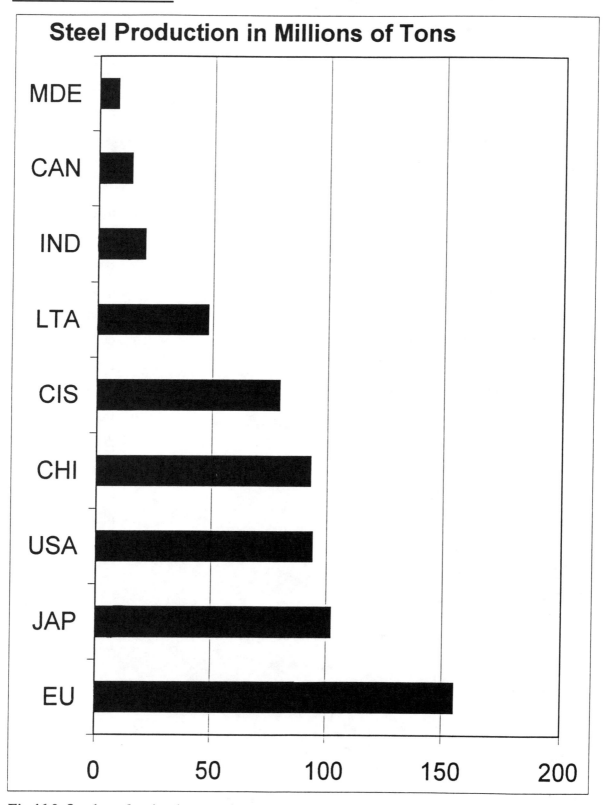

Fig 16.8. Steel production bar graph.

ACTIVITY 16 ANSWERS

a.	The Pittsburgh Pirates to the New York Yankees?	east
b.	The Boston Red Sox to the Los Angeles Dodgers?	southwest
c.	The Baltimore Orioles to the St. Louis Cardinals?	west
d.	The Montreal Expos to the Florida Marlins (Miami)?	south
e.	The Toronto Blue Jays to the Detroit Tigers?	southwest
f.	The Philadelphia Phillies to the Seattle Mariners?	northwest
g.	The Atlanta Braves to the Chicago Cubs?	northwest
h.	The New York Mets and the Tampa Bay Devil Rays?	1,138 miles
i.	The Milwaukee Brewers and the Minnesota Twins (Minneapolis)?	338 miles
j.	The Cincinnati Reds and the Colorado Rockies (Denver)?	1,168 miles
k.	The Kansas City Royals and the San Diego Padres?	1,601 miles
l.	The Oakland Athletics and the San Francisco Giants?	8 miles
m.	The Cleveland Indians and the Anaheim Angels?	2,366 miles
n.	The Houston Astros to the Chicago White Sox?	1,085 miles

ACTIVITY 22 ANSWERS

a.	The baseball team in the story	Pirates
b.	An enclosed chamber for melting iron ore	furnace
c.	A building where steel was made	mill
d.	A strong metal used for making cars	steel
e.	Molten iron was poured from this container	thimble
f.	Leftovers from the process of melting iron	slag
g.	Transportation used to go in and out of the mill	train
h.	It signaled that it was time to stop working	whistle
i.	The period of time that each man worked	shift
j.	It kept Dad's coffee hot	thermos
k.	It could pick up heavy equipment	crane
l.	A bar of steel	ingot
m.	Where the baseball team played	Forbes Field
n.	A tall container for helping smoke escape	smokestack
o.	The story took place near this city	Pittsburgh
p.	Thimbles poured out a liquid called _____ _____	molten iron

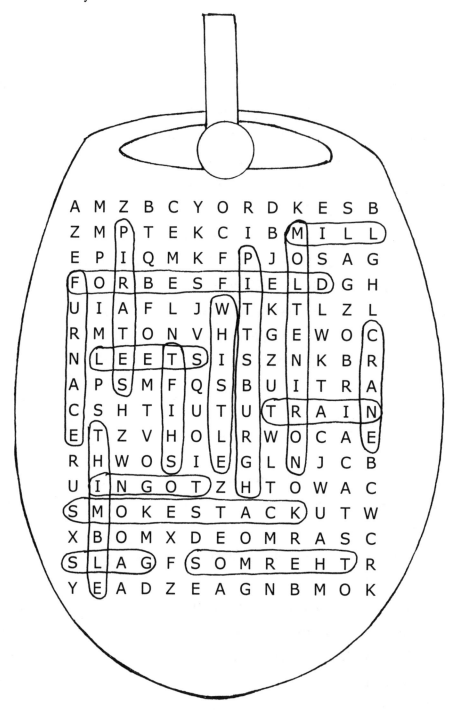

Fig. 16.9. Word Search—*No Star Nights*.

Chapter 14—*Just a Dream*

ACTIVITY 16 ANSWERS

Renewable Resources	Nonrenewable Resources
cotton	air
cows	coal
electricity (water-generated)	copper
fish	diamonds
glass	electricity (coal-generated)
ocean tides	gasoline
paper	iron ore
plastic	natural gas
trees	petroleum
wheat	soil
wind	water
wool	

ACTIVITY 17 ANSWERS

Across

1. "Every litter bit _____" — hurts
3. If it is _____, it will decompose in the environment — biodegradable
6. To rot — decay
8. To use foolishly; trash or garbage — waste
11. The act of saving; not wasting — conservation
13. Paper and trash scattered along streets and roads — litter
14. The study of relationships between organisms and the environment — ecology
15. Impurities in environment — pollution

Down

1. The place where an organism lives — habitat
2. They often pollute the air — factories
4. The act of rotting or decaying — decomposition
5. Species in danger of becoming extinct are called _____ — endangered
7. All that surrounds someone or something — environment
9. An ecological community — ecosystem
10. Trash; often found in outer space, as well — junk
12. To reuse — recycle

Fig. 16.10. Crossword—*Just a Dream.*

Chapter 15—*The Wump World*

ACTIVITY 5 ANSWERS

Wumps	Pollutians
frightened	adventuresome
nonheroic	aggressive
passive	frenzied
peaceful	greedy
timid	overjoyed

ACTIVITY 17 ANSWERS

a. I am a tiny planet, smaller than Earth, with no oceans, mountains, or broad deserts. — Wump World

b. We are simple grass-eaters who spend most of our time grazing on the tall, slender grass. — the Wumps

c. I am an old worn-out planet from which the Pollutians left. — Pollutus

d. We are beings who develop lands without concern for the future. — the Pollutians

e. I am the leader of the Pollutians. — the World Chief

f. I am the national symbol of the Pollutians. I appear on their flag. — three smokestacks

g. We are what the Wumps ate underground. — mushrooms and green moss

h. We are special trees that the Wumps love to nibble. — bumbershoot trees

i. We are what the Pollutians put into the streams and rivers. — waste, trash, pollution

j. We are what the Pollutians put into the air. — smoke, fumes, pollution

k. We are the three beings who coordinated the Pollutians' travel. — the Outer Spacemen

l. I am where the Pollutians came after they left the Wump World. — a bigger and better world

Index

About the Authors

The Butzows live in Indiana, Pennsylvania, a small University town located in rural western Pennsylvania. One room of their home houses an extensive collection of children's and adolescent literature that provides the basis for the research involved in selecting books and developing instructional ideas included in their four books on the use of literature in elementary and middle school instruction.

Carol and John both have undergraduate degrees from St. Bonaventure University in New York State. In addition, Carol completed master's degrees in history from Colgate University and in reading education from the University of Maine. Carol's doctoral degree in elementary education was earned at Indiana University of Pennsylvania. John's master's degree was earned at St. Bonaventure, and his doctorate in science education came from the University of Rochester. Carol has many years of experience teaching at the middle-junior high level, as well as at the college level. John originally worked as a teacher of science and university science educator and more recently has been a university administrator.

John and Carol have traveled extensively throughout the United States, including Alaska, to present workshops, inservice courses, and conferences. They have also spoken to audiences in Canada, Scotland, and Sweden. For information on workshops or conference presentations, please contact them through Libraries Unlimited.